THE PELICAN SHAKESPEARE
GENERAL EDITORS

STEPHEN ORGEL
A. R. BRAUNMULLER

The Life of Timon of Athens

Spranger Barry as Timon, from Bell's
edition of Shakespeare, 1776

William Shakespeare

———

The Life of
Timon of Athens

EDITED BY FRANCES E. DOLAN

PENGUIN BOOKS

PENGUIN BOOKS
An imprint of Penguin Random House LLC
penguinrandomhouse.com

The Life of Timon of Athens edited by Charlton Hinman published in
Penguin Books (USA) 1964
Revised edition published 1982
Edition edited by Frances E. Dolan published 2000
This edition published 2020

ISBN 978-0-14-071487-6

Printed in the United States of America
Set in Adobe Garamond
Designed by Virginia Norey

Contents

Publisher's Note

THE PELICAN SHAKESPEARE has served generations of readers as an authoritative series of texts and scholarship since the first volume appeared under the general editorship of Alfred Harbage over half a century ago. In the past decades, new editions followed to reflect the profound changes textual and critical studies of Shakespeare have undergone. The texts of the plays and poems were thoroughly revised in accordance with leading scholarship, and in some cases were entirely reedited. New introductions and notes were provided in all the volumes. The Pelican Shakespeare was designed as a successor to the original series; the previous editions had been taken into account, and the advice of the previous editors was solicited where it was feasible to do so. The current editions include updated bibliographic references to recent scholarship.

Certain textual features of the new Pelican Shakespeare should be particularly noted. All lines are numbered that contain a word, phrase, or allusion explained in the glossarial notes. In addition, for convenience, every tenth line is also numbered, in italics when no annotation is indicated. The intrusive and often inaccurate place headings inserted by early editors are omitted (as has become standard practice), but for the convenience of those who miss them, an indication of locale now appears as the first item in the annotation of each scene.

In the interest of both elegance and utility, each speech prefix is set in a separate line when the speakers' lines are in verse, except when those words form the second half of a verse line. Thus the verse form of the speech is kept visually intact. What is printed as verse and what is printed as prose has, in general, the authority of the original texts. Departures from the original texts in this regard have the authority only of editorial tradition and the judgment of the Pelican editors; and, in a few instances, are admittedly arbitrary.

The Theatrical World

Economic realities determined the theatrical world in which Shakespeare's plays were written, performed, and received. For centuries in England, the primary theatrical tradition was nonprofessional. Craft guilds (or "mysteries") provided religious drama – mystery plays – as part of the celebration of religious and civic festivals, and schools and universities staged classical and neoclassical drama in both Latin and English as part of their curricula. In these forms, drama was established and socially acceptable. Professional theater, in contrast, existed on the margins of society. The acting companies were itinerant; playhouses could be any available space – the great halls of the aristocracy, town squares, civic halls, inn yards, fair booths, or open fields – and income was sporadic, dependent on the passing of the hat or on the bounty of local patrons. The actors, moreover, were considered little better than vagabonds, constantly in danger of arrest or expulsion.

In the late 1560s and 1570s, however, English professional theater began to gain respectability. Wealthy aristocrats fond of drama – the Lord Admiral, for example, or the Lord Chamberlain – took acting companies under their protection so that the players technically became members of their households and were no longer subject to arrest as homeless or masterless men. Permanent theaters were first built at this time as well, allowing the companies to control and charge for entry to their performances.

Shakespeare's livelihood, and the stunning artistic explosion in which he participated, depended on pragmatic and architectural effort. Professional theater requires ways to restrict access to its offerings; if it does not, and admission fees cannot be charged, the actors do not get paid, the costumes go to a pawnbroker, and there is no such thing as a professional, ongoing theatrical tradition. The answer to that economic need arrived in the late 1560s and 1570s with the creation of the so-called public or amphitheater playhouse. Recent discoveries indicate that the precursor of the Globe playhouse in London (where Shakespeare's mature plays were presented) and the Rose theater (which presented Christopher Marlowe's plays and some of Shakespeare's earliest ones) was the Red Lion theater of 1567. Archaeological studies of the foundations of the Rose and Globe theaters have revealed that the open-air theater of the 1590s and later was probably a polygonal building with fourteen to twenty or twenty-four sides, multistoried, from 75 to 100 feet in diameter, with a raised, partly covered "thrust" stage that projected into a group of standing patrons, or "groundlings," and a covered gallery, seating up to 2,500 or more (very crowded) spectators.

These theaters might have been about half full on any given day, though the audiences were larger on holidays or when a play was advertised, as old and new were, through printed playbills posted around London. The metropolitan area's late-Tudor, early-Stuart population (circa 1590–1620) has been estimated at about 150,000 to 250,000. It has been supposed that in the mid-1590s there were about 15,000 spectators per week at the public theaters; thus, as many as 10 percent of the local population went to the theater regularly. Consequently, the theaters' repertories – the plays available for this experienced and frequent audience – had to change often: in the month between September 15 and October 15, 1595, for instance, the Lord Admiral's Men performed twenty-eight times in eighteen different plays.

Since natural light illuminated the amphitheaters' stages, performances began between noon and two o'clock and ran without a break for two or three hours. They often concluded with a jig, a fencing display, or some other nondramatic exhibition. Weather conditions determined the season for the amphitheaters: plays were performed every day (including Sundays, sometimes, to clerical dismay) except during Lent – the forty days before Easter – or periods of plague, or sometimes during the summer months when law courts were not in session and the most affluent members of the audience were not in London.

To a modern theatergoer, an amphitheater stage like that of the Rose or Globe would appear an unfamiliar mixture of plainness and elaborate decoration. Much of the structure was carved or painted, sometimes to imitate marble; elsewhere, as under the canopy projecting over the stage, to represent the stars and the zodiac. Appropriate painted canvas pictures (of Jerusalem, for example, if the play was set in that city) were apparently hung on the wall behind the acting area, and tragedies were accompanied by black hangings, presumably something like crepe festoons or bunting. Although these theaters did not employ what we would call scenery, early modern spectators saw numerous large props, such as the "bar" at which a prisoner stood during a trial, the "mossy bank" where lovers reclined, an arbor for amorous conversation, a chariot, gallows, tables, trees, beds, thrones, writing desks, and so forth. Audiences might learn a scene's location from a sign (reading "Athens," for example) carried across the stage (as in Bertolt Brecht's twentieth-century productions). Equally captivating (and equally irritating to the theater's enemies) were the rich costumes and personal props the actors used: the most valuable items in the surviving theatrical inventories are the swords, gowns, robes, crowns, and other items worn or carried by the performers.

Magic appealed to Shakespeare's audiences as much as it does to us today, and the theater exploited many deceptive and spectacular devices. A winch in the loft above the stage, called "the heavens," could lower and raise actors playing gods, goddesses, and other supernatural figures to and from the main acting area, just as one or more trap-doors permitted entrances and exits to and from the area, called "hell," beneath the stage. Actors wore elementary makeup such as wigs, false beards, and face paint, and they employed pigs' bladders filled with animal blood to make wounds seem more real. They had rudimentary but effective ways of pretending to behead or hang a person. Supernumeraries (stagehands or actors not needed in a particular scene) could make thunder sounds (by shaking a metal sheet or rolling an iron ball down a chute) and show lightning (by blowing inflammable resin through tubes into a flame). Elaborate fireworks enhanced the ef-fects of dragons flying through the air or imitated such ce-lestial phenomena as comets, shooting stars, and multiple suns. Horses' hoofbeats, bells (located perhaps in the tower above the stage), trumpets and drums, clocks, can-non shots and gunshots, and the like were common sound effects. And the music of viols, cornets, oboes, and recorders was a regular feature of theatrical performances.

For two relatively brief spans, from the late 1570s to 1590 and from 1599 to 1614, the amphitheaters com-peted with the so-called private, or indoor, theaters, which originated as, or later represented themselves as, educational institutions training boys as singers for church services and court performances. These indoor theaters had two features that were distinct from the am-phitheaters': their personnel and their playing spaces. The amphitheaters' adult companies included both adult men, who played the male roles, and boys, who played the female roles; the private, or indoor, theater companies, on the other hand, were entirely composed of boys aged about 8 to 16, who were, or could pretend to be, can-didates for singers in a church or a royal boys' choir. (Until 1660, professional theatrical companies included no women.) The playing space would appear much more familiar to modern audiences than the long-vanished amphitheaters; the later indoor theaters were, in fact, the ancestors of the typical modern theater. They were enclosed spaces, usually rectangular, with the stage filling one end of the rectangle and the audience arrayed in seats or benches across (and sometimes lining) the building's longer axis. These spaces staged plays less frequently than the public theaters (perhaps only once a week) and held far fewer spectators than the amphitheaters: about 200 to 600, as opposed to 2,500 or more. Fewer patrons mean a smaller gross income, unless each pays more. Not surprisingly, then, private theaters charged higher prices than the amphitheaters, probably sixpence, as opposed to a penny for the cheapest entry.

Protected from the weather, the indoor theaters presented plays later in the day than the amphitheaters, and used artificial illumination – candles in sconces or candelabra. But candles melt, and need replacing, snuffing, and trimming, and these practical requirements may have been part of the reason the indoor theaters introduced breaks in the performance, the intermission so dear to the heart of theatergoers and to the pocketbooks of theater concessionaires ever since. Whether motivated by the need to tend to the candles or by the entrepreneurs' wishing to sell oranges and liquor, or both, the indoor theaters eventually established the modern convention of the noncontinuous performance. In the early modern "private" theater, musical performances apparently filled the intermissions, which in Stuart theater jargon seem to have been called "acts."

At the end of the first decade of the seventeenth century, the distinction between public amphitheaters and private indoor companies ceased. For various cultural, political, and economic reasons, individual companies gained control of both the public, open-air theaters and the indoor ones, and companies mixing adult men and boys took over the formerly "private" theaters. Despite the death of the boys' companies and of their highly innovative theaters (for which such luminous playwrights as Ben Jonson, George Chapman, and John Marston wrote), their playing spaces and conventions had an immense impact on subsequent plays: not merely for the intervals (which stressed the artistic and architectonic importance of "acts"), but also because they introduced political and social satire as a popular dramatic ingredient, even in tragedy, and a wider range of actorly effects, encouraged by their more intimate playing spaces.

Even the briefest sketch of the Shakespearean theatrical world would be incomplete without some comment on the social and cultural dimensions of theaters and playing in the period. In an intensely hierarchical and status-conscious society, professional actors and their ventures had hardly any respectability; as we have indicated, to protect themselves against laws designed to curb vagabondage and the increase of masterless men, actors resorted to the near-fiction that they were the servants of noble masters, and wore their distinctive livery. Hence the company for which Shakespeare wrote in the 1590s that called itself the Lord Chamberlain's Men and pretended that the public, money-getting performances were in fact rehearsals for private performances before that high court official. From 1598, the Privy Council had licensed theatrical companies, and after 1603, with the accession of King James I, the companies gained explicit royal protection, just as the Queen's Men had for a time under Queen Elizabeth. The Chamberlain's Men became the King's Men, and the other companies were patronized by the other members of the royal family.

These designations were legal fictions that half-concealed an important economic and social development, the evolution away from the theater's organization on the model of the guild, a self-regulating confraternity of individual artisans, into a proto-capitalist organization. Shakespeare's company became a joint-stock company, where persons who supplied capital and, in some cases, such as Shakespeare's, capital and talent, employed themselves and others in earning a return on that capital. This development meant that actors and theater companies were outside both the traditional guild structures, which required some form of civic or royal charter, and the feudal household organization of master-and-servant. This anomalous, maverick social and economic condition made theater companies practically unruly and potentially even dangerous; consequently, numerous official bodies – including the London metropolitan and ecclesiastical authorities as well as, occasionally, the royal court itself – tried, without much success, to control and even to disband them.

Public officials had good reason to want to close the theaters: they were attractive nuisances – they drew often riotous crowds, they were always noisy, and they could be politically offensive and socially insubordinate. Until the Civil War, however, anti-theatrical forces failed to shut down professional theater, for many reasons – limited surveillance and few police powers, tensions or outright hostilities among the agencies that sought to check or channel theatrical activity, and lack of clear policies for control. Another reason must have been the theaters' undeniable popularity. Curtailing any activity enjoyed by such a substantial percentage of the population was difficult, as various Roman emperors attempting to limit circuses had learned, and the Tudor-Stuart audience was not merely large, it was socially diverse and included women. The prevalence of public entertainment in this period has been underestimated. In fact, fairs, holidays, games, sporting events, the equivalent of modern parades, freak shows, and street exhibitions all abounded, but the theater was the most widely and frequently available entertainment to which people of every class had access. That fact helps account both for its quantity and for the fear and anger it aroused.

Books About Shakespeare's Theater

Useful scholarly studies of theatrical life in Shakespeare's day include: G. E. Bentley, *The Jacobean and Caroline Stage*, 7 vols. (1941–68), and the same author's *The Professions of Dramatist and Player in Shakespeare's Time, 1590–1642* (1986); Julian Bowsher, *The Rose Theatre: An Archaeological Discovery* (1998); E. K. Chambers, *The Elizabethan Stage*, 4 vols. (1923); Christine Eccles, *The Rose Theatre* (1990); R. A. Foakes, *Illustrations of the English Stage, 1580–1642* (1985); Andrew Gurr, *The Shakespearean Stage, 1574–1642*, 3rd ed. (1992), and the same author's *Playgoing in Shakespeare's London*, 2nd ed. (1996); Roslyn Lander Knutson, *Playing Companies and Commerce in Shakespeare's Time* (2001); Edwin Nungezer, *A Dictionary of Actors* (1929); Carol Chillington Rutter, ed., *Documents of the Rose Playhouse* (1984); Tiffany Stern, *Documents of Performance in Early Modern England* (2009); Glynne Wickham, Herbert Berry, and William Ingram, *English Professional Theatre, 1530–1660* (2009).

WILLIAM SHAKESPEARE OF
STRATFORD-UPON-AVON, GENTLEMAN

Many people have said that we know very little about William Shakespeare's life – pinheads and postcards are often mentioned as appropriately tiny surfaces on which to record the available information. More imaginatively and perhaps more correctly, Ralph Waldo Emerson wrote, "Shakespeare is the only biographer of Shakespeare. . . . So far from Shakespeare's being the least known, he is the one person in all modern history fully known to us."

In fact, we know more about Shakespeare's life than we do about almost any other English writer's of his era. His last will and testament (dated March 25, 1616) survives, as do numerous legal contracts and court documents involving Shakespeare as principal or witness, and parish records in Stratford and London. Shakespeare appears quite often in official records of King James's royal court, and of course Shakespeare's name appears on numerous title pages and in the written and recorded words of his literary contemporaries Robert Greene, Henry Chettle, Francis Meres, John Davies of Hereford, Ben Jonson, and many others. Indeed, if we make due allowance for the bloating of modern, run-of-the-mill bureaucratic records, more information has survived over the past four hundred years about William Shakespeare of Stratford-upon-Avon, Warwickshire, than is likely to survive in the next four hundred years about any reader of these words.

What we do not have are entire categories of information – Shakespeare's private letters or diaries, drafts and revisions of poems and plays, critical prefaces or essays, commendatory verse for other writers' works, or instructions guiding his fellow actors in their performances, for instance – that we imagine would help us understand and appreciate his surviving writings. For all we know, many such data never existed as written records. Many literary and theatrical critics, not knowing what might once have existed, more or less cheerfully accept the situation; some even make a theoretical virtue of it by claiming that such data are irrelevant to understanding and interpreting the plays and poems.

So, what do we know about William Shakespeare, the man responsible for thirty-seven or perhaps more plays, more than 150 sonnets, two lengthy narrative poems, and some shorter poems?

While many families by the name of Shakespeare (or some variant spelling) can be identified in the English Midlands as far back as the twelfth century, it seems likely that the dramatist's grandfather, Richard, moved to Snitterfield, a town not far from Stratford-upon-Avon, sometime before 1529. In Snitterfield, Richard Shakespeare leased farmland from the very wealthy Robert Arden. By

1552, Richard's son John had moved to a large house on Henley Street in Stratford-upon-Avon, the house that stands today as "The Birthplace." In Stratford, John Shakespeare traded as a glover, dealt in wool, and lent money at interest; he also served in a variety of civic posts, including "High Bailiff," the municipality's equivalent of mayor. In 1557, he married Robert Arden's youngest daughter, Mary. Mary and John had four sons – William was the oldest – and four daughters, of whom only Joan outlived her most celebrated sibling. William was baptized (an event entered in the Stratford parish church records) on April 26, 1564, and it has become customary, without any good factual support, to suppose he was born on April 23, which happens to be the feast day of Saint George, patron saint of England, and is also the date on which he died, in 1616. Shakespeare married Anne Hathaway in 1582, when he was eighteen and she was twenty-six; their first child was born five months later. It has been generally assumed that the marriage was enforced and subsequently unhappy, but these are only assumptions; it has been estimated, for instance, that up to one third of Elizabethan brides were pregnant when they married. Anne and William Shakespeare had three children: Susanna, who married a prominent local physician, John Hall; and the twins Hamnet, who died young in 1596, and Judith, who married Thomas Quiney – apparently a rather shady individual. The name Hamnet was unusual but not unique: he and his twin sister were named for their godparents, Shakespeare's neighbors Hamnet and Judith Sadler. Shakespeare's father died in 1601 (the year of *Hamlet*), and Mary Arden Shakespeare died in 1608 (the year of *Coriolanus*). William Shakespeare's last surviving direct descendant was his granddaughter Elizabeth Hall, who died in 1670.

Between the birth of the twins in 1585 and a clear reference to Shakespeare as a practicing London dramatist in Robert Greene's sensationalizing, satiric pamphlet, *Greene's Groatsworth of Wit* (1592), there is no record of where

William Shakespeare was or what he was doing. These seven so-called lost years have been imaginatively filled by scholars and other students of Shakespeare: some think he traveled to Italy, or fought in the Low Countries, or studied law or medicine, or worked as an apprentice actor/writer, and so on to even more fanciful possibilities. Whatever the biographical facts for those "lost" years, Greene's nasty remarks in 1592 testify to professional envy and to the fact that Shakespeare already had a successful career in London. Speaking to his fellow playwrights, Greene warns both generally and specifically:

> . . . trust them [actors] not: for there is an upstart crow, beautified with our feathers, that with his tiger's heart wrapped in a player's hide supposes he is as well able to bombast out a blank verse as the best of you; and being an absolute Johannes Factotum, is in his own conceit the only Shake-scene in a country.

The passage mimics a line from *3 Henry VI* (hence the play must have been performed before Greene wrote) and seems to say that "Shake-scene" is both actor and playwright, a jack-of-all-trades. That same year, Henry Chettle protested Greene's remarks in *Kind-Heart's Dream*, and each of the next two years saw the publication of poems – *Venus and Adonis* and *The Rape of Lucrece*, respectively – publicly ascribed to (and dedicated by) Shakespeare. Early in 1595 he was named as one of the senior members of a prominent acting company, the Lord Chamberlain's Men, when they received payment for court performances during the 1594 Christmas season.

Clearly, Shakespeare had achieved both success and reputation in London. In 1596, upon Shakespeare's application, the College of Arms granted his father the now-familiar coat of arms he had taken the first steps to obtain almost twenty years before, and in 1598, John's son – now permitted to call himself "gentleman" – took a

10 percent share in the new Globe playhouse. In 1597, he bought a substantial bourgeois house, called New Place, in Stratford – the garden remains, but Shakespeare's house, several times rebuilt, was torn down in 1759 – and over the next few years Shakespeare spent large sums buying land and making other investments in the town and its environs. Though he worked in London, his family remained in Stratford, and he seems always to have considered Stratford the home he would eventually return to. Something approaching a disinterested appreciation of Shakespeare's popular and professional status appears in Francis Meres's *Palladis Tamia* (1598), a not especially imaginative and perhaps therefore persuasive record of literary reputations. Reviewing contemporary English writers, Meres lists the titles of many of Shakespeare's plays, including one not now known, *Love's Labor's Won*, and praises his "mellifluous & hony-tongued" "sugred Sonnets," which were then circulating in manuscript (they were first collected in 1609). Meres describes Shakespeare as "one of the best" English playwrights of both comedy and tragedy. In *Remains . . . Concerning Britain* (1605), William Camden – a more authoritative source than the imitative Meres – calls Shakespeare one of the "most pregnant witts of these our times" and joins him with such writers as Chapman, Daniel, Jonson, Marston, and Spenser. During the first decades of the seventeenth century, publishers began to attribute numerous play quartos, including some non-Shakespearean ones, to Shakespeare, either by name or initials, and we may assume that they deemed Shakespeare's name and supposed authorship, true or false, commercially attractive.

For the next ten years or so, various records show Shakespeare's dual career as playwright and man of the theater in London, and as an important local figure in Stratford. In 1608-9 his acting company – designated the "King's Men" soon after King James had succeeded Queen Elizabeth in 1603 – rented, refurbished, and opened a small interior playing space, the Blackfriars theater, in London, and Shakespeare was once again listed as a substantial sharer in the group of proprietors of the playhouse. By May 11, 1612, however, he describes himself as a Stratford resident in a London lawsuit – an indication that he had withdrawn from day-to-day professional activity and returned to the town where he had always had his main financial interests. When Shakespeare bought a substantial residential building in London, the Blackfriars Gatehouse, close to the theater of the same name, on March 10, 1613, he is recorded as William Shakespeare "of Stratford upon Avon in the county of Warwick, gentleman," and he named several London residents as the building's trustees. Still, he continued to participate in theatrical activity: when the new Earl of Rutland needed an allegorical design to bear as a shield, or *impresa,* at the celebration of King James's Accession Day, March 24, 1613, the earl's accountant recorded a payment of 44 shillings to Shakespeare for the device with its motto.

For the last few years of his life, Shakespeare evidently concentrated his activities in the town of his birth. Most of the final records concern business transactions in Stratford, ending with the notation of his death on April 23, 1616, and burial in Holy Trinity Church, Stratford-upon-Avon.

THE QUESTION OF AUTHORSHIP

The history of ascribing Shakespeare's plays (the poems do not come up so often) to someone else began, as it continues, peculiarly. The earliest published claim that someone else wrote Shakespeare's plays appeared in an 1856 article by Delia Bacon in the American journal *Putnam's Monthly* – although an Englishman, Thomas Wilmot, had shared his doubts in private (even secretive) conversations with friends near the end of the eighteenth century. Bacon's was a sad personal history that ended in madness and poverty, but the year after her article, she published, with great difficulty and the bemused assistance of Nathaniel Hawthorne (then United States Consul in Liverpool, England), her *Philosophy of the Plays of Shakspere Unfolded*. This huge, ornately written, confusing farrago is almost unreadable; sometimes its intents, to say nothing of its arguments, disappear entirely beneath near-raving, ecstatic writing. Tumbled in with much supposed "philosophy" appear the claims that Francis Bacon (from whom Delia Bacon eventually claimed descent), Walter Raleigh, and several other contemporaries of Shakespeare's had written the plays. The book had little impact except as a ridiculed curiosity.

Once proposed, however, the issue gained momentum among people whose conviction was the greater in proportion to their ignorance of sixteenth- and seventeenth-century English literature, history, and society. Another American amateur, Catharine F. Ashmead Windle, made the next influential contribution to the cause when she published *Report to the British Museum* (1882), wherein she promised to open "the Cipher of Francis Bacon," though what she mostly offers, in the words of S. Schoenbaum, is "demented allegorizing." An entire new cottage industry grew from Windle's suggestion that the texts contain hidden, cryptographically discoverable ciphers – "clues" – to their authorship; and today there are not only books devoted to the putative ciphers, but also pamphlets, journals, and newsletters.

Although Baconians have led the pack of those seeking a substitute Shakespeare, in *"Shakespeare" Identified* (1920), J. Thomas Looney became the first published "Oxfordian" when he proposed Edward de Vere, seventeenth earl of Oxford, as the secret author of Shakespeare's plays. Also for Oxford and his "authorship" there are today dedicated societies, articles, journals, and books. Less popular candidates – Queen Elizabeth and Christopher Marlowe among them – have had adherents, but the movement seems to have divided into two main contending factions, Baconian and Oxfordian. (For further details on all the candidates for "Shakespeare," see S. Schoenbaum, *Shakespeare's Lives,* 2nd ed., 1991.)

The Baconians, the Oxfordians, and supporters of other candidates have one trait in common – they are snobs. Every pro-Bacon or pro-Oxford tract sooner or later claims that the historical William Shakespeare of Stratford-upon-Avon could not have written the plays because he could not have had the training, the university education, the experience, and indeed the imagination or background their author supposedly possessed. Only a learned genius like Bacon or an aristocrat like Oxford could have written such fine plays. (As it happens, lucky male children of the middle class had access to better education than most aristocrats in Elizabethan England – and Oxford was not particularly well educated.) Shakespeare received in the Stratford grammar school a formal education that would daunt many college graduates today; and popular rival playwrights such as the very learned Ben Jonson and George Chapman, both of whom also lacked university training, achieved great artistic success, without being taken as Bacon or Oxford.

Besides snobbery, one other quality characterizes the authorship controversy: lack of evidence. A great deal of testimony from Shakespeare's time shows that Shakespeare wrote Shakespeare's plays and that his contemporaries recognized them as distinctive and distinctly superior. (Some of that contemporary evidence is collected in E. K. Chambers, *William Shakespeare: A Study of Facts and Problems,* 2 vols., 1930.) Since that testimony comes from Shakespeare's enemies and theatrical competitors as well as from his co-workers and from the Elizabethan equivalent of literary journalists, it seems unlikely that, if any of these sources had known he was a fraud, they would have failed to record that fact.

Books About Shakespeare's Life

The following books provide scholarly, documented accounts of Shakespeare's life: G. E. Bentley, *Shakespeare: A Biographical Handbook* (1961); E. K. Chambers, *William Shakespeare: A Study of Facts and Problems*, 2 vols. (1930); S. Schoenbaum, *William Shakespeare: A Compact Documentary Life* (1977), and the same author's *Shakespeare's Lives*, 2nd ed. (1991); James Shapiro, *Contested Will: Who Wrote Shakespeare?* (2010). Many scholarly editions of Shakespeare's complete works print brief compilations of essential dates and events. References to Shakespeare's works up to 1700 are collected in C. M. Ingleby et al., *Shakespeare Allusion-Book*, rev. ed., 2 vols. (1932).

The Texts of Shakespeare

As FAR AS WE KNOW, only one manuscript conceivably in Shakespeare's own hand may (and even this is much disputed) exist: a few pages of a play called *Sir Thomas More*, which apparently was never performed. What we do have, as later readers, performers, scholars, students, are printed texts. The earliest of these survive in two forms: quartos and folios. Quartos (from the Latin for "four") are small books, printed on sheets of paper that were then folded twice, to make four leaves or eight pages. When these were bound together, the result was a squarish, eminently portable volume that sold for the relatively small sum of sixpence (translating in modern terms to about $5). In folios, on the other hand, the sheets are folded only once, in half, producing large, impressive volumes taller than they are wide. This was the format for important works of philosophy, science, theology, and literature (the major precedent for a folio Shakespeare was Ben Jonson's *Works*, 1616). The decision to print the works of a popular playwright in folio is an indication of how far up on the social scale the theatrical profession had come during Shakespeare's lifetime. The Shakespeare folio was an expensive book, selling for between fifteen and eighteen shillings, depending on the binding (in modern terms, from about $150 to $180). Twenty Shakespeare plays of the thirty-seven that survive first appeared in quarto, seventeen of which appeared during Shakespeare's lifetime; the rest of the plays are found only in folio.

The First Folio was published in 1623, seven years after Shakespeare's death, and was authorized by his fellow actors, the co-owners of the King's Men. This publication was certainly a mark of the company's enormous respect for Shakespeare; but it was also a way of turning the old plays, most of which were no longer current in the playhouse, into ready money (the folio includes only Shakespeare's plays, not his sonnets or other nondramatic verse). Whatever the motives behind the publication of the folio, the texts it preserves constitute the basis for almost all later editions of the playwright's works. The texts, however, differ from those of the earlier quartos, sometimes in minor respects but often significantly – most strikingly in the two texts of *King Lear,* but also in important ways in *Hamlet, Othello,* and *Troilus and Cressida.* (The variants are recorded in the textual notes to each play in the new Pelican series.) The differences in these texts represent, in a sense, the essence of theater: the texts of plays were initially not intended for publication. They were scripts, designed for the actors to perform – the principal life of the play at this period was in performance. And it follows that in Shakespeare's theater the playwright typically had no say either in how his play was performed or in the disposition of his text – he was an employee of the company. The authoritative figures in the theatrical enterprise were the shareholders in the company, who were for the most part the major actors. They decided what plays were to be done; they hired the playwright and often gave him an outline of the play they wanted him to write. Often, too, the play was a collaboration: the company would retain a group of writers, and parcel out the scenes among them. The resulting script was then the property of the company, and the actors would revise it as they saw fit during the course of putting it on stage. The resulting text belonged to the company. The playwright had no rights in it once he had been paid. (This system survives largely intact in the movie industry, and most of the playwrights of Shakespeare's time were as anonymous as most screenwriters are today.) The script could also, of course, continue to change as the tastes of audiences and the requirements of the actors changed. Many – perhaps most – plays were revised when they were reintroduced after any substantial absence from the repertory, or when they were performed by a company different from the one that originally commissioned the play.

Shakespeare was an exceptional figure in this world because he was not only a shareholder and actor in his company, but also its leading playwright – he was literally his own boss. He had, moreover, little interest in the publication of his plays, and even those that appeared during his lifetime with the authorization of the company show no signs of any editorial concern on the part of the author. Theater was, for Shakespeare, a fluid and supremely responsive medium – the very opposite of the great classic canonical text that has embodied his works since 1623.

The very fluidity of the original texts, however, has meant that Shakespeare has always had to be edited. Here is an example of how problematic the editorial project inevitably is, a passage from the most famous speech in *Romeo and Juliet,* Juliet's balcony soliloquy beginning "O Romeo, Romeo, wherefore art thou Romeo?" Since the eighteenth century, the standard modern text has read,

> What's Montague? It is nor hand, nor foot,
> Nor arm, nor face, nor any other part
> Belonging to a man. O be some other name!
> What's in a name? That which we call a rose
> By any other name would smell as sweet.
>
> (II.2.40–44)

Editors have three early texts of this play to work from, two quarto texts and the folio. Here is how the First Quarto (1597) reads:

> Whats *Mountague* ? It is nor band nor foote,
> Nor arme, nor face, nor any other parr.
> Whats in a name? That which we call a Rose,
> By any other name would smell as sweet:

Here is the Second Quarto (1599):

> Whats *Mountague* ? it is nor hand nor foote,
> Nor arme nor face, ô be some other name
> Belonging to a man.
> Whats in a name that which we call a rose,
> By any other word would smell as sweete,

And here is the First Folio (1623):

> What's *Mountague* ? it is nor hand nor foote,
> Nor arme, nor face, O be some other name
> Belonging to a man.
> What ? in a names that which we call a Rose,
> By any other word would smell as sweete,

There is in fact no early text that reads as our modern text does – and this is the most famous speech in the play. Instead, we have three quite different texts, all of which are clearly some version of the same speech, but none of which seems to us a final or satisfactory version. The transcendently beautiful passage in modern editions is an editorial invention: editors have succeeded in conflating and revising the three versions into something we recognize as great poetry. Is this what Shakespeare "really" wrote? Who can say? What we can say is that Shakespeare always had performance, not a book, in mind.

Books About the Shakespeare Texts

The standard study of the printing history of the First Folio is W. W. Greg, *The Shakespeare First Folio* (1955). J. K. Walton, *The Quarto Copy for the First Folio of Shakespeare* (1971), is a useful survey of the relation of the quartos to the folio. The second edition of Charlton Hinman's *Norton Facsimile* of the First Folio (1996), with a new introduction by Peter Blayney, is indispensable. Stanley Wells, Gary Taylor, John Jowett, and William Montgomery, *William Shakespeare: A Textual Companion,* keyed to the Oxford text, gives a comprehensive survey of the editorial situation for all the plays and poems.

Introduction

CRITICAL DEBATES ABOUT *Timon of Athens* are almost as contentious and irresolvable as Timon's spats with the visitors to his cave in Act IV. There is no consensus about the play's date, although it is often placed between 1605 and 1608-10. Various hypotheses attempt to explain what many find to be an incoherent or unsatisfying play by relieving Shakespeare of some of the responsibility for the finished (or unfinished) product (see Note on the Text). By whatever means *Timon of Athens* achieved the form in which it comes to us, it is a challenge to those who seek to prise a coherent interpretation from it. For others, this is precisely what makes the play interesting.

The play is organized around a central character, his actions and transformation, and other characters' reactions to him. This is typical of Shakespeare's tragedies, all of which are named after their heroes. Yet *Timon* sports a surfeit of commentators on the central figure: the poet, who describes Timon and his situation to us before we meet him; the cynical malcontent Apemantus, who must eventually compete with Timon for the monopoly on misanthropy; the loyal steward, Flavius; the somewhat superfluous fool. All reflect on Timon and his fortunes.

Yet Timon, the focus of their attentions, and the center of the play, is not at all a stable figure. True, the protagonists of Shakespeare's other tragedies also change in the course of their plays. But Timon splits abruptly into two. First he is the gift giver, whose generosity secures a large and attentive entourage. "How this lord is followed!" (I.1.39) the painter marvels; the steward wonders, "Who is not Timon's?" (II.2.168). Yet when Timon's money has been spent, his friends or followers depart, and with them goes the person Timon has been. Timon the benefactor becomes Timon the curser; he christens his new persona with a new name, Misanthropos. While these two

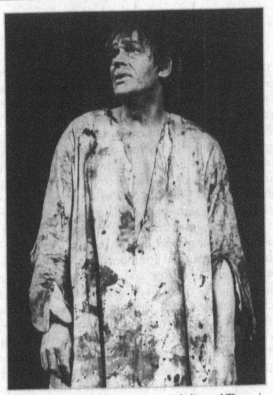

The great Paul Scofield as an intense and alienated Timon in John Schlesinger's production for the Royal Shakespeare Company, 1965.

Timons share characteristics – both are aggressive, immoderate, and domineering – the world and the play, like Timon's character, are transformed by Timon's decline in fortunes. The play charts this sudden and disorienting lurch from wealth to poverty, from benevolence to bitterness, from Timon's urban mansion to his rural cave, from giving gifts to hurling abuse. Briefly, the two Timons and the two worlds overlap: when Timon parodies his own earlier banquets by serving his false friends stones and hot water – "Uncover, dogs, and lap" (III.6.86) – he combines hospitality with hostility. In this last "feast" at the mansion, he reveals it to be as barren as his cave will be; the stones in covered dishes are even less appetizing than the roots for which Timon will later dig.

Because Timon, like his friends, changes with his fortunes, the play can be seen as a case study of how circumstances shape, even determine, identity. The second senator, for instance, describes how Timon's experience constructs his character.

> At all times alike
> Men are not still the same. 'Twas time and griefs
> That framed him thus. Time, with his fairer hand
> Offering the fortunes of his former days,
> The former man may make him.
>
> (V.1.120-24)

The first senator argues that, over time, social construction becomes second nature. If Timon lives too long as Misanthropos, then the earlier Timon (of Athens) will be irrecoverable: "His discontents are unremovably / Coupled to nature" (V.1.223-24). The abrupt and extreme change in Timon suggests that identity is not stable, nor is it separate from or able to transcend adversity. We do not "make our own luck." Our luck makes us; identity is an effect of fortune.

The first senator advises that one must never internalize misfortune, that one must wear it on the sleeve, not in the heart:

> He's truly valiant that can wisely suffer
> The worst that man can breathe, and make his
>   wrongs
> His outsides, to wear them like his raiment, care-
>   lessly,

> And ne'er prefer his injuries to his heart,
> To bring it into danger.
>
> (III.5.31-35)

The senator advises a stoical, but also a theatrical, disregard for suffering, as if one could keep one's self separate from and unaffected by it. This is not a standard that Timon, whose loss and grief radically transform him from the inside out, can meet.

Alcibiades, the military leader who is banished by the Athenian Senate when he pleads for the life of one of his men, similarly changes in response to changed circumstances. This figure has a historical precedent, a skilled, popular, and ambitious general banished by the Athenian Senate in the fifth century B.C., who then in retaliation collaborated with Athens' greatest enemy, Sparta. Many histories of Athens, beginning with that by Thucydides, depict both the Senate's poor judgment in estranging a brilliant military tactician and Alcibiades' own subsequent treason as turning points in Athens' military and imperial decline. In Shakespeare's play, Timon and Alcibiades offer contrasting responses to Athenian ingratitude. Both characters view their disappointment and betrayal in terms of an unfair exchange or a bad bargain. Alcibiades, for instance, argues that the Senate has paid him for his valor in wounds rather than wages:

> I'm worse than mad: I have kept back their foes
> While they have told their money and let out
> Their coin upon large interest, I myself
> Rich only in large hurts. All those for this?
>
> (III.5.105-8)

His response is to use his martial prowess against rather than on behalf of the Senate. The relationship between Timon and Alcibiades is one site of incoherence in the play; the relationship between the two and Athens is another. In what way was Alcibiades' war against Athens "In part for his [Timon's] sake moved" (V.2.13)? Why does Timon turn against Alcibiades, who himself is driven to ask, "Why me, Timon?" (IV.3.106). How could Timon have helped Athens in its "great peril" even if he had been willing to return? What was his value to a military effort as a person or presence? Although these details are difficult to sort out, Timon and Alcibiades stand as two different figures for Athens' failure, and, consequently, its division against itself. The Senate banishes Alcibiades; Timon banishes himself.

Both Timon and Alcibiades construe their relationships in economic terms, lamenting the inadequate return they receive on their investments, the ingratitude of those they have served, the failure of reciprocity. Yet the economic is not just a language or a figure for more abstract social relations. The play is also intensely interested in the accumulation and circulation of wealth, presenting two distinct, yet overlapping, economic systems. At first, Timon presides over a gift economy in which he gains prestige through unreciprocal generosity, not through exchange. As Timon explains, "there's none / Can truly say he gives, if he receives" (I.2.10-11). Another kind of economy exists beneath or beside this one. As Timon's money runs out, a new vocabulary emerges: "bonds," "uses," "bills," "forfeiture," "engaged." As it turns out, for instance, Timon borrowed money of Lucius, which he then returned to him as jewels or gifts. Thus a loan underpinned and enabled the gift economy. If Timon incurred debts to the very men whom he would not allow to reciprocate his "gifts," then the two economies are not really distinct. Furthermore, some of his gifts are in cash, but a "cash" that is only fuzzily explained. The currency includes "pieces," "crowns," "solidares," and "talents," the value of which is uncertain. Five and three talents seem like large gifts from Timon to Ventidius and Lucilius, respectively (I.1.95, 141); yet Timon himself subsequently requests fifty and a thousand (II.2.194-95, 201; III.1.17). Sometimes the text does not even specify amounts, suggesting just "so many." This vagueness compounds the impression that the precise amount is not the point. What, then, is? What is the play saying about gifts, money, generosity, and exchange?

Timon of Athens gestures toward different attitudes to money and wealth: between those who have acquired it recently and those who have inherited it; between those who earn wages (like Alcibiades and his soldiers, Timon's servants, and the women who will "do anything for gold," IV.3.150) and those whose wealth is attained mysteriously offstage; between masters and servants, high and low. Timon's sudden bankruptcy shatters many of these distinctions, demonstrating that his wealth, too, has a source and a limit. He is not so different from the prostitutes he abuses. By what means did Timon acquire the wealth that he then redistributes with such abandon? What difference would knowing the source of that wealth make to our evaluation of how and why Timon spends it?

Timon's steward offers an alternative both to Timon's excessive generosity and to the stinginess of his false friends. Sharing his meager reserves with other servants seems a more meaningful act than Timon's grandiose, thoughtless expenditures. The steward also stands apart from the play's wage earners, for he presents himself as driven by loyalty and love, not by a salary. In his willingness to follow his master and help him even in adversity, the steward earns a place in the pantheon of loyal servants in Shakespeare's plays. But his loyalty does not guarantee that his assessment of Timon is correct. Is it true that Timon was "Undone by goodness" (IV.2.38)? While Timon, like Christ, sacrifices himself and is betrayed by his followers, the parallels between the two are deeply troubling. For Timon cannot even save himself. Indeed, he becomes an anti-Christ who tries to curse and condemn as many others as possible.

Many have found a resemblance between *Timon* and *King Lear*. Coleridge, for instance, described the play as "a Lear of the satirical Drama, a Lear of domestic and ordinary Life – a local Eddy of Passion on the High Road of

Society while all around is the week-day Goings on of Wind and Weather – a Lear therefore without its soul-scorching flashes."* While the life depicted in *Timon of Athens* hardly seems ordinary, there are fascinating connections between the two heroes. Both give gifts in the expectation that they will be repaid with love and loyalty; both are scandalized and maddened by ingratitude; both escape the disappointments of the household to the freedom and misery of being "unhoused"; both escalate from disappointment in specific people to a more wide-ranging disappointment in humanity. For Timon, as for Lear, a disordered and fallen world is one turned upside down, in which broken obligations, disrupted reciprocity, diseased sexuality, and "confounding contraries" predominate (IV.1.20). Yet Timon desires this chaos, since it would be a more accurate manifestation of what he has come to view as the "truth" about humans and their relationships. Timon insists that among humans and animals, there is always a hierarchy. He has moved from the top to the bottom, but the structure itself has not changed.

Timon's misogyny is not as specific or as vivid as the misogyny expressed by Hamlet, Othello, or Lear, all of whom curse a particular woman who they think has betrayed them and then proceed to condemn women more generally. Yet Timon, too, reveals the crucial role misogyny plays in misanthropy. He attacks Timandra and Phrynia as more destructive than war; he describes gold as a whore because it infects and debases men; he directs less abuse at the thieves than he does at these two women (IV.3). This is a play in which there are no female characters, except for the unnamed "ladies" (I.2) who say little and Alcibiades' companions, whom Timon calls "a brace of harlots" (IV.3.80).

---

* Samuel Taylor Coleridge, *Lectures 1808–1819 on Literature,* ed. R. A. Foakes (Princeton: Princeton University Press, 1987), Bollingen Series LXXV, vol. 5, pt. 2 of *The Collected Works of Samuel Taylor Coleridge,* gen. ed. Kathleen Coburn, 16 vols., p. 376.

Although women in this play have no power, little presence, and few lines, Timon relentlessly abuses them as the origin or symbol of what's wrong with humankind. The misogyny here hardly needs women to sustain itself; indeed, it can proceed unchecked in their absence.

Like Lear, Timon rants with imagination and vigor. Yet he is pettier than Lear. Furthermore, Timon's critique does not neatly correspond to his own experience. Timon finds in misanthropy a passion and commitment that he has not revealed before. Since Timon recovers his wealth almost immediately when, digging for roots to eat, he finds gold, he must freely choose to sustain his misanthropy and isolation. He does. This counters Apemantus's charge that Timon does not adopt his "sour cold habit" to "castigate [his] pride" but rather does it "enforcedly" (IV.3.239–41). Although the gold makes Timon no longer a beggar, he does not choose to return to Athens. His discovery of the gold suggests one way in which Timon of Athens and Misanthropos are not so very different. In both personae, in both halves of the play, Timon views wealth as a burden: he needs to bestow it on others, to get rid of it. Throughout, he is a giver of gifts. In the second half of the play, he is more openly hostile, and his conditions are more explicit. For instance, Timon's gift to the steward is only on the condition that he suppress his own judicious generosity and "Hate all, curse all, show charity to none" (IV.3.525).

Timon dies offstage; his death stands at multiple removes, not only from the audience but also from the Athenians to whom it will mean most. Furthermore, Alcibiades' invasion of Athens and compromise with the senators dominates the play's close, and pushes Timon to the margins. We are not invited to care about how Timon dies or about his experience of death. Denying Timon the significance usually invested in the death of the tragic hero, the play raises a final question about its own genre. Is it a tragedy? A satire? A morality play? The confusion surrounding Timon's epitaph suggests just how difficult it is to understand what the "last word" on him is, what the perspective is from which we can best understand his story. Although Timon advises his steward to turn to his gravestone as an "oracle," the gravestone compounds rather than alleviates confusion (V.1.217). Timon has two epitaphs, one in an undescribed form (paper? stone?) in English, which the soldier reads, and another engraved in stone, apparently in Latin or some other language that the soldier cannot read, and which he can convey only by making a wax impression. Why include this detail? The play highlights the unreliable and mediated processes by which information is transmitted, knowledge created, history recorded. The wax impression also suggests that the recording and transmission of information do not necessarily require comprehension. As it happens, the epitaph that the soldier cannot read is more discussed than the one that he can; the wax impression is a more reliable and concrete record than his memory of the more accessible epitaph. Furthermore, both of the epitaphs are presented to the audience in English; apparently, Alcibiades translates the impression of the second epitaph as he reads it.

The process of "copying" and translating the epitaph does not, however, bring Alcibiades, the senators, or the audience to the heart of Timon's mystery. For this second epitaph is actually two, which seem to speak in different voices. The first couplet instructs the reader, "Seek not my name"; the second explains, "Here lie I, Timon." In large part, these warring couplets can be explained as undigested source material. In composing *Timon*, Shakespeare may have drawn on the Greek satirist Lucian's dialogue *Timon the Misanthrope*, for which an English translation was not available; on William Painter's *The Palace of Pleasure* (1566), a compendium of prose tales in English collected out of classical and Italian sources, from which Shakespeare often borrowed; or on another Elizabethan play about Timon, which has come to be known as the "academic" or "old" *Timon*. It is less disputed that Shakespeare consulted

Sir Thomas North's English translation of a French translation of Plutarch's *Lives of the Noble Grecians and Romanes*,
as he had in composing his Roman plays, *Julius Caesar,
Coriolanus,* and *Antony and Cleopatra.* Written in Greek in
the first century A.D., Plutarch's text appeared in North's
translation in 1579 and 1595. Plutarch records two epitaphs, "Here lie I," written by a poet about Timon, and
"Seek not my name," written by Timon himself and engraved on his tomb. Shakespeare records the two, presenting them as parts of one whole. Yet the two different voices
and perspectives speak against, and cancel or confuse, one
another. The contradiction goes even deeper. For all his
contempt for others, Timon seems to have spent his last
hours composing various epitaphs in two languages, and
engraving them onto his own tombstone. Surely, this is a
curious enterprise for one who wishes to sink into obscu-
rity, and who has no regard for the attention or opinion of
others. The epitaphs demand attention, and then curse
those who have stopped to read them. Perhaps Shakespeare
intended to strike out one of the two couplets in the second
epitaph, but never got around to it. That they stand together with no bridge across the gap between them seems a
fitting "epitaph" not only for Timon/Misanthropos, but
also for a play that has often been viewed as broken, as two
distinct halves not quite soldered together.

FRANCES E. DOLAN
Miami University, Ohio

Note on the Text

No QUARTO, OR SINGLE-TEXT, edition of *Timon of Athens* survives; the play was first printed in the First Folio of 1623. While many disputes about Shakespearean texts emerge from the disparities between quarto and folio versions of the plays, in this case the folio version itself raises questions. These begin with the play's inclusion and position in the First Folio. *Timon* immediately follows *Romeo and Juliet.* Yet some copies of the folio include a leaf with the last page of *Romeo and Juliet* and the first page of *Troilus and Cressida.* This leaf, which offers a glimpse into changes made during the printing process, suggests that *Troilus* was first slated to stand as the fourth of the tragedies. When difficulties arose, perhaps over copyright on *Troilus and Cressida, Timon* was used to fill the spot. Was it moved there from elsewhere in the volume, in a shuffling rather than a change in the table of contents? Or was it not, at first, scheduled for inclusion? If not, why not? These uncertainties have suggested to some that *Timon of Athens* was on the margins of the Shakespeare canon, and that, as a consequence, its claims on our attention are lesser or more troubled than those of some of the other plays.

A suspicion that *Timon of Athens* is not quite or not fully "Shakespearean" corresponds to various theories about its authorship and the reasons for its textual problems. The text provokes speculation because some features suggest that it is unfinished. These features include: irregular spellings of names and inconsistent naming of some characters (for example, in the list of actors' names and in II.2 and III.4, servants seem to be called by their masters' names; Flavius, in I.2, seems to become the steward thereafter; a ghost character, the mercer in I.1 who is announced in the stage direction, then says nothing); untimely entrances (characters whose arrival is announced long before they play any role in the action, as with the painter and poet, IV.3.349); false exits (characters who seem to leave, then are called upon); metrical problems (passages intermixing prose, rhymed couplets, and blank verse, lines with too many or too few syllables to scan).

Various theories attempt to explain these contradictions and inconsistencies, and, especially, to shift blame from Shakespeare. John Heminges and Henry Condell, who prepared the folio for publication, claimed in their epistle addressed "To the great variety of readers" that Shakespeare's "mind and hand went together: And what he thought, he uttered with that easiness, that we have scarce received from him a blot in his papers." This oft-repeated claim that Shakespeare was above revision has come under considerable pressure. The folio text of *Timon,* which reproduces "blots," has led some to argue that if Shakespeare did not revise, he should have. Many critics have expressed disappointment in the play, especially in the shift that occurs in the middle, seeming to cleave the play into two incompatible halves. All the available arguments for accounting for imperfect play texts have been used in reference to *Timon of Athens:* it is an unrevised draft, which was never performed and which Shakespeare may have abandoned; it is an incomplete or unintegrated collaboration between Shakespeare and another playwright, with any parts found inadequate usually assigned to the other writer (most recently, Thomas Middleton); although it is the work of one author, the transcript was prepared by two hands, the author's and a professional scribe's; it is another writer's botched revision or adaptation of a Shakespearean play; it is an actor's patchy transcript from memory of a play in which he appeared, but for which he did not have a complete text; it is finished, and the only failure is ours, not the play's or the playwright's. Since it is impossible to know the process by which the play achieved its shape, this edition tries not to erase or explain away the inconsistencies.

Like most editions, this one regularizes the spelling of names, modernizes and standardizes spelling and punctuation, relineates the text, presenting some passages set as prose in the folio text as verse, and provides act and scene divisions to aid study and discussion. It also adds some new stage directions or clarifications of existing stage directions, signaling these with brackets. While this edition does not reproduce many "corrections" that gained currency among eighteenth-century editors and have been accepted since, those few substantive changes that are listed below generally follow generations of editorial practice. The adopted reading in italics is followed by the folio reading in roman.

The Actors' Names (printed at the end of the play in F)

I.1 21 *gum . . . oozes* Gowne . . . uses 87 *hands . . . slip* hand . . . sit 166 *satiety* society 213 *cost* cast 224 *feigned* fegin'd 249 *there* their 276 *Come* Comes

I.2 148 *LADY* 1 Lord 222 *Ay* I

II.2 4 *resumes* resume 74, 102 *mistress'* Masters 94 *Ay. Would* I would 130 *proposed* propose 137 *found* sound 157 *of* or 187 *Flaminius* Flavius

III.2 38 *fifty–five hundred* fifty five hundred

III.3 21 *and I* and

III.4 112 *Sempronius* Sempronius Ullorxa

III.5 17 *An* And 63 *I say* say 67 *'em* him

III.6 19 *here's* heares 47 *Servants bring in the banquet, then leave* The banquet brought in [at 40 in F] 81 *lag* legge 91 *with your* you with

IV.1 6 *steads* steeds 13 *Son* Some

IV.2 41 *does* do

IV.3 3 *Twinned* Twin'd 10 *senator* Senators 12 *pasture* Pastour 13 *lean* leave 15 *say* fay 88 *tub fast* fub-fast 117 *window bars* window Barne 156 *scolds* scold'st 255 *command* command'st 380 *son and sire* Sunne and fire 392 *to shortly* too shortly; *Thronged to?* Throng'd too 395 *them* then 432 *villainy* Villaine 472 *grant'st* grunt'st 507 *A* If not a

V.1 50 *worship* worshipt 69 *men* man 125 *chance* chanc'd 146 *sense* since 181 *reverend'st* reverends

V.4 44 *all together* altogether 55 *Descend* Defend

The Life of
Timon of Athens

THE ACTORS' NAMES

TIMON OF ATHENS
LUCIUS
LUCULLUS } *flattering lords*
SEMPRONIUS
VENTIDIUS, *one of Timon's false friends*
APEMANTUS, *a churlish philosopher*
ALCIBIADES, *an Athenian captain*
[FLAVIUS, *steward to Timon*]
POET, PAINTER, JEWELER, MERCHANT [, MERCER]
[AN OLD ATHENIAN]
FLAMINIUS
[LUCILIUS] } *Timon's servants*
SERVILIUS
CAPHIS
PHILOTUS
TITUS } *several servants [to Timon's creditors]*
HORTENSIUS
[OTHERS]
[A PAGE]
[A FOOL]
[THREE STRANGERS]
[PHRYNIA } *mistresses to Alcibiades*]
[TIMANDRA
CERTAIN MASKERS [AS] CUPID [AND AMAZONS]
[LORDS, LADIES,] SENATORS, [OFFICERS,
    MESSENGERS, SOLDIERS,] THIEVES, SERVANTS
    [TO LUCIUS AND LUCULLUS], AND ATTENDANTS

[SCENE: *Athens, and the woods nearby*]

*

The Life of
Timon of Athens

I.1 *Enter Poet, Painter, Jeweler, Merchant, and
Mercer, at several doors.*

POET
  Good day, sir.
PAINTER   I am glad you're well.
POET
  I have not seen you long; how goes the world?   2
PAINTER
  It wears, sir, as it grows.   3
POET   Ay, that's well known.
  But what particular rarity? What strange,
  Which manifold record not matches? See,   5
  Magic of bounty, all these spirits thy power   6
  Hath conjured to attend! I know the merchant.
PAINTER
  I know them both. Th' other's a jeweler.
MERCHANT
  O, 'tis a worthy lord!
JEWELER   Nay, that's most fixed.   9

I.1 The house of Timon, Athens **s.d.** *Mercer* a dealer in fabrics and notions
(this character does not speak, nor is he acknowledged, in this scene) **2** *long*
for a long time **3** *wears . . . grows* wears out as it ages **5** *manifold . . .
matches* is unmatched in all history **6** *bounty* generosity **9** *fixed* certain

MERCHANT

10   A most incomparable man; breathed, as it were,

11   To an untirable and continuate goodness.

12   He passes.

JEWELER   I have a jewel here –

MERCHANT

      O, pray let's see't. For the Lord Timon, sir?

JEWELER

14   If he will touch the estimate; but for that –

POET   *[Recites.]*

15   "When we for recompense have praised the vile,
      It stains the glory in that happy verse
      Which aptly sings the good."

MERCHANT   *[Looks at the jewel.]* 'Tis a good form.

JEWELER

18   And rich. Here is a water, look ye.

PAINTER

19   You are rapt, sir, in some work, some dedication

20   To the great lord.

POET   A thing slipped idly from me.

21   Our poesy is as a gum which oozes
      From whence 'tis nourished. The fire i' th' flint
      Shows not till it be struck; our gentle flame

24   Provokes itself and like the current flies
      Each bound it chases. What have you there?

PAINTER

      A picture, sir. When comes your book forth?

POET

27   Upon the heels of my presentment, sir.
      Let's see your piece.

---

10 *breathed* trained (through exercise)   11 *continuate* enduring   12 *passes* excels   14 *touch the estimate* meet the price   15–17 *When . . . good* i.e., false praise lowers the value of poetry that praises truly   18 *water* luster   19 *rapt* engrossed   21–24 *Our poesy . . . itself* i.e., poetry runs spontaneously from its source, needing no external stimulus   21 *gum* sap   24 *Provokes* lights, in-spires   24–25 *flies . . . chases* shrinks from each riverbank it seemed to pur-sue   27 *presentment* presentation of it (to Timon)

PAINTER   'Tis a good piece.

POET
So 'tis. This comes off well and excellent.

PAINTER
Indifferent.   30

POET   Admirable. How this grace
Speaks his own standing! What a mental power   31
This eye shoots forth! How big imagination
Moves in this lip! To th' dumbness of the gesture   33
One might interpret.   34

PAINTER
It is a pretty mocking of the life.
Here is a touch; is't good?

POET   I will say of it,
It tutors nature. Artificial strife   37
Lives in these touches, livelier than life.
      Enter certain Senators [and pass over].

PAINTER
How this lord is followed!

POET
The senators of Athens. Happy men!   40

PAINTER
Look, more!

POET
You see this confluence, this great flood of visitors:
I have in this rough work shaped out a man
Whom this beneath world doth embrace and hug
With amplest entertainment. My free drift   45
Halts not particularly, but moves itself   46
In a wide sea of wax; no leveled malice
Infects one comma in the course I hold,   48

---

31 *Speaks . . . standing* expresses the worth of its subject   33 *Moves in* is suggested by; *dumbness* speechlessness   34 *interpret* find words   37 *Artificial strife* the struggle of art to outdo nature   45 *entertainment* welcome; *drift* aim   46 *particularly* on any individual   46–48 *moves . . . wax* i.e., has great scope (though *wax* has not been altogether satisfactorily explained)   48 *comma* i.e., detail

49   But flies an eagle flight, bold and forth on,
50   Leaving no tract behind.
PAINTER
51   How shall I understand you?
POET   I will unbolt to you.
52   You see how all conditions, how all minds,
         As well of glib and slipp'ry creatures as
54   Of grave and austere quality, tender down
         Their services to Lord Timon. His large fortune,
         Upon his good and gracious nature hanging,
57   Subdues and properties to his love and tendance
58   All sorts of hearts; yea, from the glass-faced flatterer
         To Apemantus, that few things loves better
60   Than to abhor himself – even he drops down
         The knee before him and returns in peace
         Most rich in Timon's nod.
PAINTER   I saw them speak together.
POET
         Sir, I have upon a high and pleasant hill
64   Feigned Fortune to be throned. The base o' th' mount
65   Is ranked with all deserts, all kind of natures
         That labor on the bosom of this sphere
67   To propagate their states. Amongst them all
         Whose eyes are on this sovereign lady fixed
69   One do I personate of Lord Timon's frame,
70   Whom Fortune with her ivory hand wafts to her,
71   Whose present grace to present slaves and servants
72   Translates his rivals.
PAINTER   'Tis conceived to scope.
         This throne, this Fortune, and this hill, methinks,

---

49 *flies* my course is   50 *tract* trace, track   51 *unbolt* open, explain   52 *conditions* social levels   54 *tender down* hand over   57 *properties* appropriates; *tendance* care, service   58 *glass-faced* reflecting like a mirror rather than transparent   64 *Feigned* depicted   65 *ranked . . . deserts* filled with men of all degrees of merit   67 *propagate . . . states* increase their fortunes   69 *personate* represent   70 *wafts* beckons   71 *to present* immediately to   72 *Translates* transforms, changes; *to scope* to the purpose or point

With one man beckoned from the rest below,
Bowing his head against the steepy mount
To climb his happiness, would be well expressed   76
In our condition.

POET   Nay, sir, but hear me on.
All those which were his fellows but of late
(Some better than his value) on the moment
Follow his strides, his lobbies fill with tendance,   80
Rain sacrificial whisperings in his ear,   81
Make sacred even his stirrup, and through him   82
Drink the free air.   83

PAINTER   Ay, marry, what of these?

POET
When Fortune in her shift and change of mood
Spurns down her late beloved, all his dependents,
Which labored after him to the mountain's top
Even on their knees and hands, let him slip down,
Not one accompanying his declining foot.

PAINTER
'Tis common.
A thousand moral paintings I can show   90
That shall demonstrate these quick blows of Fortune's
More pregnantly than words. Yet you do well   92
To show Lord Timon that mean eyes have seen   93
The foot above the head.

*Trumpets sound. Enter Lord Timon, addressing
himself courteously to every suitor [; a Messenger
from Ventidius talking with him; Lucilius and other
Servants following].*

TIMON   Imprisoned is he, say you?

76–77 *would . . . condition* would be closely paralleled by our situation in
the real world   80 *lobbies . . . tendance* crowd his house to attend on him
81 *sacrificial* worshipful   82–83 *through . . . air* act as if indebted to him
even for breathing   83 *marry* to be sure (originally an oath on the name of
the Virgin Mary)   90 *moral* allegorical   92 *pregnantly* fully, creatively   93
mean lowly

MESSENGER

95 Ay, my good lord. Five talents is his debt,
96 His means most short, his creditors most strait.
Your honorable letter he desires
To those have shut him up, which failing
99 Periods his comfort.

TIMON   Noble Ventidius! Well,

100 I am not of that feather to shake off
My friend when he must need me. I do know him
A gentleman that well deserves a help,
Which he shall have. I'll pay the debt and free him.

MESSENGER

104 Your lordship ever binds him.

TIMON

Commend me to him. I will send his ransom;
106 And, being enfranchised, bid him come to me.
'Tis not enough to help the feeble up,
But to support him after. Fare you well.

MESSENGER

All happiness to your honor!   *Exit.*
        Enter an old Athenian.

OLD MAN

110 Lord Timon, hear me speak.

TIMON   Freely, good father.

OLD MAN

Thou hast a servant named Lucilius.

TIMON

I have so. What of him?

OLD MAN

Most noble Timon, call the man before thee.

TIMON

Attends he here or no? Lucilius!

---

95 *talents* large units of silver or gold, sometimes valued at several thousand dollars each (in *Timon*, the apparent value seems to vary enormously) 96 *strait* exacting, strict 99 *Periods* ends 100 *feather* kind, character 104 *binds* attaches by ties of gratitude (but with quibble on *free* in l. 103) 106 *enfranchised* freed 110 *father* (respectful form of address to an old man)

LUCILIUS

    Here, at your lordship's service.

OLD MAN

    This fellow here, Lord Timon, this thy creature,   116
    By night frequents my house. I am a man
    That from my first have been inclined to thrift,   118
    And my estate deserves an heir more raised
    Than one which holds a trencher.   120

TIMON   Well; what further?

OLD MAN

    One only daughter have I, no kin else
    On whom I may confer what I have got.
    The maid is fair, o' th' youngest for a bride,   123
    And I have bred her at my dearest cost   124
    In qualities of the best. This man of thine   125
    Attempts her love. I prithee, noble lord,   126
    Join with me to forbid him her resort;   127
    Myself have spoke in vain.

TIMON   The man is honest.

OLD MAN

    Therefore he will be, Timon.
    His honesty rewards him in itself;   *130*
    It must not bear my daughter.   131

TIMON   Does she love him?

OLD MAN

    She is young and apt.   132
    Our own precedent passions do instruct us
    What levity's in youth.

TIMON   Love you the maid?

LUCILIUS

    Ay, my good lord, and she accepts of it.

---

116 *creature* dependent (contemptuous)   118 *first* earliest days, youth   120 *holds a trencher* i.e., waits table   123 *o' th' youngest for* barely old enough to be   124 *bred* brought up, educated   125 *qualities* accomplishments   126 *Attempts* seeks to win   127 *her resort* access to her   129 *will be* i.e., will act honestly (and stop pursuing my daughter against my wishes)   131 *bear* win   132 *apt* impressionable

OLD MAN
    If in her marriage my consent be missing,
    I call the gods to witness I will choose
    Mine heir from forth the beggars of the world
139   And dispossess her all.

TIMON   How shall she be endowed
140   If she be mated with an equal husband?

OLD MAN
    Three talents on the present; in future, all.

TIMON
    This gentleman of mine hath served me long;
    To build his fortune I will strain a little,
144   For 'tis a bond in men. Give him thy daughter:
    What you bestow, in him I'll counterpoise,
    And make him weigh with her.

OLD MAN   Most noble lord,
147   Pawn me to this your honor, she is his.

TIMON
    My hand to thee; mine honor on my promise.

LUCILIUS
    Humbly I thank your lordship. Never may
150   That state or fortune fall into my keeping
151   Which is not owed to you!
                        Exit [Lucilius, with old Athenian].

POET   *[Presents his poem.]*
152   Vouchsafe my labor, and long live your lordship!

TIMON
153   I thank you; you shall hear from me anon.
    Go not away. – What have you there, my friend?

PAINTER
    A piece of painting, which I do beseech
    Your lordship to accept.

---

139 *all* wholly   144 *bond* obligation   147 *Pawn . . . honor* if you'll pledge,
on your honor, to do so   151 *owed* (acknowledged as) due   152 *Vouchsafe*
deign to accept   153 *anon* soon

TIMON   Painting is welcome.
  The painting is almost the natural man;   157
  For since dishonor traffics with man's nature
  He is but outside; these penciled figures are   159
  Even such as they give out. I like your work,   160
  And you shall find I like it. Wait attendance
  Till you hear further from me.
PAINTER   The gods preserve ye!
TIMON
  Well fare you, gentleman. Give me your hand;
  We must needs dine together. – Sir, your jewel
  Hath suffered under praise.   165
JEWELER   What, my lord? Dispraise?
TIMON
  A mere satiety of commendations.
  If I should pay you for't as 'tis extolled,
  It would unclew me quite.   168
JEWELER   My lord, 'tis rated
  As those which sell would give; but you well know   169
  Things of like value, differing in the owners,   170
  Are prizèd by their masters. Believe't, dear lord,   171
  You mend the jewel by the wearing it.
TIMON
  Well mocked.   173
    Enter Apemantus.
MERCHANT
  No, my good lord; he speaks the common tongue
  Which all men speak with him.
TIMON   Look who comes here.
  Will you be chid?   176

157–60 *The painting . . . out* i.e., painting can almost be said to represent
what man is instead of what he pretends to be 159 *penciled* painted 165
suffered under been overwhelmed with (complimentary, but the jeweler takes
it otherwise) 168 *unclew* ruin (undo, as in unwinding a ball of yarn) 169
As . . . give i.e., at cost 171 *by* according to 173 *mocked* pretended,
feigned

176 JEWELER   We'll bear, with your lordship.

MERCHANT
He'll spare none.

TIMON
Good morrow to thee, gentle Apemantus.

APEMANTUS
179 Till I be gentle stay thou for thy good morrow —
180 When thou art Timon's dog, and these knaves honest.

TIMON
Why dost thou call them knaves? Thou know'st them
not.

APEMANTUS   Are they not Athenians?

TIMON   Yes.

APEMANTUS   Then I repent not.

JEWELER   You know me, Apemantus?

APEMANTUS   Thou know'st I do; I called thee by thy
name.

TIMON   Thou art proud, Apemantus.

APEMANTUS   Of nothing so much as that I am not like
190 Timon.

TIMON   Whither art going?

APEMANTUS   To knock out an honest Athenian's brains.

TIMON   That's a deed thou'lt die for.

APEMANTUS   Right, if doing nothing be death by th' law.

TIMON   How lik'st thou this picture, Apemantus?

196 APEMANTUS   The best for the innocence.

TIMON   Wrought he not well that painted it?

APEMANTUS   He wrought better that made the painter,
and yet he's but a filthy piece of work.

200 PAINTER   You're a dog.

201 APEMANTUS   Thy mother's of my generation. What's she,
if I be a dog?

TIMON   Wilt dine with me, Apemantus?

---

176 *We'll ... lordship* i.e., we can stand it if you can   179 *stay ... morrow*
expect such greeting from me   180 *When ... honest* i.e., never   196 *innocence* silliness   201 *generation* breed, species

APEMANTUS   No, I eat not lords.

TIMON   An thou shouldst, thou'dst anger ladies.   205

APEMANTUS   O, they eat lords. So they come by great   206
bellies.

TIMON   That's a lascivious apprehension.   208

APEMANTUS   So thou apprehend'st it; take it for thy
labor.   210

TIMON   How dost thou like this jewel, Apemantus?

APEMANTUS   Not so well as plain-dealing, which will not
cost a man a doit.   213

TIMON   What dost thou think 'tis worth?

APEMANTUS   Not worth my thinking. How now, poet?

POET   How now, philosopher?

APEMANTUS   Thou liest.

POET   Art not one?

APEMANTUS   Yes.

POET   Then I lie not.   220

APEMANTUS   Art not a poet?

POET   Yes.

APEMANTUS   Then thou liest. Look in thy last work,   223
where thou hast feigned him a worthy fellow.

POET   That's not feigned; he is so.

APEMANTUS   Yes, he is worthy of thee, and to pay thee
for thy labor. He that loves to be flattered is worthy o'
th' flatterer. Heavens, that I were a lord!

TIMON   What wouldst do then, Apemantus?

APEMANTUS   E'en as Apemantus does now – hate a lord   230
with my heart.

TIMON   What, thyself?

APEMANTUS   Ay.

TIMON   Wherefore?

---

205 *An* if   206 *eat* consume, engulf, have sex with   208 *apprehension* (1)
idea, (2) capture (of men by women)   213 *doit* small coin, even less valuable
than a penny   223 *Then thou liest* (because it is necessary for poets to
"feign," hence to be liars)

235 APEMANTUS   That I had no angry wit to be a lord. Art
        not thou a merchant?

MERCHANT   Ay, Apemantus.

238 APEMANTUS   Traffic confound thee, if the gods will not!

MERCHANT   If traffic do it, the gods do it.

240 APEMANTUS   Traffic's thy god; and thy god confound
        thee!

    Trumpet sounds. Enter a Messenger.

TIMON
    What trumpet's that?

MESSENGER
    'Tis Alcibiades and some twenty horse,
244 All of companionship.

TIMON
    Pray entertain them; give them guide to us.

                    [Exeunt some Attendants.]

    You must needs dine with me. Go not you hence
    Till I have thanked you. When dinner's done,
248 Show me this piece. – I am joyful of your sights.

    Enter Alcibiades with the rest.

    Most welcome, sir!

    [They salute.]

APEMANTUS   So; so; there!
250 Aches contract and starve your supple joints!
    That there should be small love amongst these sweet
        knaves,
252 And all this courtesy! The strain of man's bred out
    Into baboon and monkey.

ALCIBIADES
254 Sir, you have saved my longing, and I feed
    Most hungerly on your sight.

---

235 *had . . . lord* had, in my anger, no more sense than to wish to be a lord
(perhaps: the line may be corrupt but has not been convincingly emended)
238 *Traffic* trade   244 *of companionship* of the same party   248 *of your sights*
to see you   250 *Aches* (pronounced "aitches"); *starve* cause to wither   252
strain race; *bred out* degenerated   254 *saved my* kept me from further

TIMON   Right welcome, sir!
Ere we depart we'll share a bounteous time
In different pleasures. Pray you, let us in.
                              Exeunt [all but Apemantus].
    Enter two Lords.
FIRST LORD   What time o' day is't, Apemantus?
APEMANTUS   Time to be honest.
FIRST LORD   That time serves still.   260
APEMANTUS   The most accursèd thou that still omit'st it.
SECOND LORD   Thou art going to Lord Timon's feast?
APEMANTUS   Ay, to see meat fill knaves and wine heat
    fools.
SECOND LORD   Fare thee well, fare thee well.
APEMANTUS   Thou art a fool to bid me farewell twice.
SECOND LORD   Why, Apemantus?
APEMANTUS   Shouldst have kept one to thyself, for I
    mean to give thee none.
FIRST LORD   Hang thyself!   270
APEMANTUS   No, I will do nothing at thy bidding. Make
    thy requests to thy friend.
SECOND LORD   Away, unpeaceable dog, or I'll spurn thee
    hence!
APEMANTUS   I will fly, like a dog, the heels o' th' ass.
                                            [Exit.]
FIRST LORD
    He's opposite to humanity. Come, shall we in
    And taste Lord Timon's bounty? He outgoes
    The very heart of kindness.
SECOND LORD
    He pours it out. Plutus, the god of gold,
    Is but his steward. No meed but he repays   280
    Sevenfold above itself; no gift to him
    But breeds the giver a return exceeding
    All use of quittance.
                                                        283

---

260 *still* always   280 *meed* (1) gift, (2) merit   283 *use of quittance* customary repayment

FIRST LORD   The noblest mind he carries
   That ever governed man.
SECOND LORD   Long may he live
285   In fortunes! Shall we in?
FIRST LORD   I'll keep you company. *Exeunt.*

                              *

ᦏ **I.2** *Hautboys playing loud music. A great banquet*
      served in [,Flavius the Steward and others attending];
      and then enter Lord Timon, the States, the Athenian
      Lords, Ventidius (which Timon redeemed from prison).
      Then comes, dropping after all, Apemantus, discon-
290   *tentedly, like himself.*

VENTIDIUS
   Most honored Timon,
   It hath pleased the gods to remember my father's age
   And call him to long peace.
   He is gone happy, and has left me rich.
   Then, as in grateful virtue I am bound
6   To your free heart, I do return those talents,
   Doubled with thanks and service, from whose help
   I derived liberty.
TIMON   O, by no means,
   Honest Ventidius. You mistake my love:
10   I gave it freely ever; and there's none
   Can truly say he gives, if he receives.
12   If our betters play at that game, we must not dare
13   To imitate them; faults that are rich are fair.
VENTIDIUS
   A noble spirit!

---

285 *In fortunes* fortunate, prosperous
   I.2 The hall in Timon's house **s.d.** *Hautboys* oboes; *States* rulers of the
state, senators **6** *free* generous **12** *If* i.e., even if **13** *that are rich* i.e., in
the rich

TIMON

 Nay, my lords, ceremony was but devised at first   15
 To set a gloss on faint deeds, hollow welcomes,
 Recanting goodness, sorry ere 'tis shown;
 But where there is true friendship, there needs none.
 Pray sit. More welcome are ye to my fortunes
 Than my fortunes to me.   20
  [They sit.]

FIRST LORD

 My lord, we always have confessed it.

APEMANTUS

 Ho, ho, confessed it? Hanged it, have you not?   22

TIMON

 O, Apemantus, you are welcome.

APEMANTUS   No,
 You shall not make me welcome;
 I come to have thee thrust me out of doors.

TIMON

 Fie, thou'rt a churl; ye've got a humor there   26
 Does not become a man; 'tis much to blame.
 They say, my lords, *Ira furor brevis est;* but yon man is 28
 very angry. Go, let him have a table by himself; for he
 does neither affect company nor is he fit for't indeed. 30

APEMANTUS Let me stay at thine apperil, Timon. I come 31
to observe; I give thee warning on't.

TIMON I take no heed of thee. Thou'rt an Athenian,
therefore welcome. I myself would have no power; 34
prithee let my meat make thee silent.

APEMANTUS I scorn thy meat. 'Twould choke me; for I
should ne'er flatter thee. O you gods, what a number of

---

15 *ceremony* politeness, courtesy **22** *confessed . . . not* (bitter allusion to proverbial "confess and be hanged") **26** *humor* temperament or characteristic resulting from an excess of one of the four "humors," or fluids, in the human body: black bile (or choler), yellow bile, blood, and phlegm **28** *Ira . . . est* anger is a brief madness (Latin, from a verse epistle by Horace) **30** *affect* like, seek **31** *thine apperil* your own risk **34** *power* i.e., to keep you quiet

men eats Timon, and he sees 'em not! It grieves me to
see so many dip their meat in one man's blood; and all
40 the madness is, he cheers them up too.
I wonder men dare trust themselves with men.
42 Methinks they should invite them without knives:
Good for their meat, and safer for their lives.
There's much example for't. The fellow that sits next
him now, parts bread with him, pledges the breath of
46 him in a divided draught, is the readiest man to kill
47 him. 'T has been proved. If I were a huge man, I should
fear to drink at meals,
49 Lest they should spy my windpipe's dangerous notes.
50 Great men should drink with harness on their throats.

TIMON [To a Lord who drinks to him]
51 My lord, in heart! and let the health go round.

SECOND LORD
Let it flow this way, my good lord.

APEMANTUS Flow this way? A brave fellow! He keeps his
54 tides well. Those healths will make thee and thy state
look ill, Timon.
Here's that which is too weak to be a sinner:
Honest water, which ne'er left man i' th' mire.
This and my food are equals; there's no odds.
59 Feasts are too proud to give thanks to the gods.

Apemantus' Grace.
60 Immortal gods, I crave no pelf;
I pray for no man but myself;
62 Grant I may never prove so fond
To trust man on his oath or bond,

---

40 *cheers . . . too* encourages them as well   42 *without knives* (Elizabethan if
not ancient Athenian guests normally brought their own)   46 *divided
draught* shared drink   47 *huge* great (in rank, not physical size)   49 *my . . .
notes* indications on my throat of where my windpipe is   50 *harness* armor
51 *in heart* heartily   54 *tides* (1) tides, which *flow,* (2) times, seasons   54–
55 *Those healths . . . ill* (cf. proverbial "to drink healths is to drink sickness")
59 *Feasts* feasters   62 *fond* foolish

Or a harlot for her weeping,
Or a dog that seems a-sleeping,
Or a keeper with my freedom,   66
Or my friends, if I should need 'em.
Amen. So; fall to't;
Rich men sin, and I eat root.
  [Eats and drinks.]
Much good dich thy good heart, Apemantus!   70

TIMON   Captain Alcibiades, your heart's in the field now.

ALCIBIADES   My heart is ever at your service, my lord.

TIMON   You had rather be at a breakfast of enemies than
a dinner of friends.

ALCIBIADES   So they were bleeding new, my lord, there's
no meat like 'em; I could wish my best friend at such a
feast.

APEMANTUS   Would all those flatterers were thine enemies then, that then thou might'st kill 'em – and bid
me to 'em!   80

FIRST LORD   Might we but have that happiness, my lord,
that you would once use our hearts, whereby we might   82
express some part of our zeals, we should think ourselves for ever perfect.   84

TIMON   O no doubt, my good friends, but the gods
themselves have provided that I shall have much help
from you: how had you been my friends else? Why
have you that charitable title from thousands, did not   88
you chiefly belong to my heart? I have told more of you
to myself than you can with modesty speak in your   90
own behalf; and thus far I confirm you. O you gods,   91
think I, what need we have any friends if we should
ne'er have need of 'em? They were the most needless
creatures living, should we ne'er have use for 'em; and
would most resemble sweet instruments hung up in

---

66 *keeper* jailer   70 *dich* may it do   82 *use our hearts* put our love to the test
84 *perfect* completely happy   88 *from thousands* i.e., you alone of all the
thousands I know   91 *confirm you* vouch for your worthiness

cases, that keeps their sounds to themselves. Why, I
97 have often wished myself poorer, that I might come
nearer to you. We are born to do benefits; and what
better or properer can we call our own than the riches
100 of our friends? O what a precious comfort 'tis to have
so many like brothers commanding one another's for-
102 tunes! O joy's e'en made away ere't can be born! Mine
103 eyes cannot hold out water, methinks. To forget their
faults, I drink to you.

APEMANTUS   Thou weep'st to make them drink, Timon.

SECOND LORD
Joy had the like conception in our eyes
And at that instant like a babe sprung up.

APEMANTUS
Ho, ho! I laugh to think that babe a bastard.

THIRD LORD
I promise you, my lord, you moved me much.

110 APEMANTUS   Much!
          Sound tucket.

TIMON
What means that trump?
          Enter Servant.   How now?

SERVANT   Please you, my lord, there are certain ladies
most desirous of admittance.

TIMON   Ladies? What are their wills?

SERVANT   There comes with them a forerunner, my lord,
116 which bears that office to signify their pleasures.

TIMON   I pray let them be admitted.   *[Exit Servant.]*
          Enter Cupid.

CUPID
Hail to thee, worthy Timon, and to all
That of his bounties taste! The five best senses
120 Acknowledge thee their patron, and come freely

97–98 *come nearer to* try   102 *made away* destroyed, turned to tears   103
cannot . . . water are leaky   110 s.d. *tucket* trumpet call   116 *which . . . office* whose function is

To gratulate thy plenteous bosom. There,   121
Taste, touch, all, pleased from thy table rise;
They only now come but to feast thine eyes.

TIMON

They're welcome all; let 'em have kind admittance.
Music, make their welcome!   [Exit Cupid.]

FIRST LORD

You see, my lord, how ample you're beloved.   126
    [Music.] Enter Cupid, with the Masque of Ladies [as]
    Amazons with lutes in their hands, dancing and
    playing.

APEMANTUS

Hoy-day!
What a sweep of vanity comes this way!
They dance? They are madwomen.
Like madness is the glory of this life   130
As this pomp shows to a little oil and root.   131
We make ourselves fools to disport ourselves
And spend our flatteries to drink those men   133
Upon whose age we void it up again   134
With poisonous spite and envy.
Who lives that's not depravèd or depraves?
Who dies that bears not one spurn to their graves   137
Of their friends' gift?   138
I should fear those that dance before me now
Would one day stamp upon me. 'T has been done.   140
Men shut their doors against a setting sun.
    The Lords rise from table, with much adoring of
    Timon, and to show their loves, each single out an
    Amazon, and all dance, men with women, a lofty
    strain or two to the hautboys, and cease.

---

121 *gratulate . . . bosom* greet thy generous heart   121–23 *There . . . eyes*
(the maskers appeal only to the eyes; that is, the men may not touch them)
126 s.d. *Amazons* mythical female warriors   130 *Like* just such   131 *As . . .
shows to* in the same sense as this lavishness is when compared with; *a little . . . root* i.e., bare necessities   133 *drink* drink healths to   134 *age* old age
137 *spurn* injury, insult   138 *Of . . . gift* given them by their friends

TIMON
    You have done our pleasures much grace, fair ladies,
    Set a fair fashion on our entertainment,
144   Which was not half so beautiful and kind;
    You have added worth unto't and luster,
146   And entertained me with mine own device.
147   I am to thank you for't.

FIRST LADY
148   My lord, you take us even at the best.

APEMANTUS   Faith, for the worst is filthy, and would not
150   hold taking, I doubt me.

TIMON
    Ladies, there is an idle banquet attends you;
152   Please you to dispose yourselves.

ALL LADIES
    Most thankfully, my lord.   *Exeunt [Cupid and Ladies].*

TIMON   Flavius.

FLAVIUS
    My lord?

TIMON   The little casket bring me hither.

FLAVIUS
    Yes, my lord. *[Aside]* More jewels yet?
157   There is no crossing him in's humor;
    Else I should tell him well, i' faith I should;
159   When all's spent, he'd be crossed then, an he could.
160   'Tis pity bounty had not eyes behind,
161   That man might ne'er be wretched for his mind. *Exit.*

FIRST LORD
    Where be our men?

---

144 *was not* i.e., before you came   146 *mine own device* (apparently Timon
has himself composed the masque)   147 *am to* should and do   148 *take . . .
best* i.e., give us most generous praise   150 *hold taking* bear handling (because the "ladies" are so riddled with infectious diseases, no man would want
to "take" them); *doubt* suspect   152 *dispose yourselves* take your places   157
humor inclination (see l. 26 n.)   159 *crossed* (1) freed of debt, (2) thwarted
(as in l. 157); *an* if   161 *for his mind* because of his (generosity of) spirit

SERVANT

  Here, my lord, in readiness.

SECOND LORD

  Our horses!

    Enter Flavius [with the casket].

TIMON   O my friends, I have one word

  To say to you. Look you, my good lord,

  I must entreat you honor me so much

  As to advance this jewel; accept it and wear it,   167

  Kind my lord.

FIRST LORD

  I am so far already in your gifts –

ALL

  So are we all.   *170*

    Enter a Servant.

SERVANT

  My lord, there are certain nobles of the Senate

  Newly alighted and come to visit you.

TIMON

  They are fairly welcome.   *[Exit Servant.]*

FLAVIUS   I beseech your honor,

  Vouchsafe me a word; it does concern you near.   174

TIMON

  Near? Why then, another time I'll hear thee. I prithee

  Let's be provided to show them entertainment.

FLAVIUS   *[Aside]*

  I scarce know how.

    Enter another Servant.

SERVANT

  May it please your honor, Lord Lucius,

  Out of his free love, hath presented to you

  Four milk-white horses trapped in silver.   180

---

167 *advance* add value to (by possessing; cf. I.1. 170–71) **174** *Vouchsafe*
allow **180** *trapped in silver* with silver-mounted trappings

TIMON
  I shall accept them fairly. Let the presents
182 Be worthily entertained.   *[Exit Servant.]*
      Enter a third Servant.
                                    How now? What news?
SERVANT Please you, my lord, that honorable gentle-
      man, Lord Lucullus, entreats your company tomorrow
      to hunt with him and has sent your honor two brace of
      greyhounds.
TIMON
  I'll hunt with him; and let them be received,
  Not without fair reward.   *[Exit Servant.]*
FLAVIUS *[Aside]*   What will this come to?
  He commands us to provide and give great gifts,
190 And all out of an empty coffer;
  Nor will he know his purse, or yield me this,
  To show him what a beggar his heart is,
193 Being of no power to make his wishes good.
194 His promises fly so beyond his state
  That what he speaks is all in debt; he owes
  For every word. He is so kind that he now
197 Pays interest for't; his land's put to their books.
  Well, would I were gently put out of office
  Before I were forced out!
200 Happier is he that has no friend to feed
201 Than such that do e'en enemies exceed.
  I bleed inwardly for my lord.   *Exit.*
TIMON   You do yourselves
203 Much wrong; you bate too much of your own merits.
  Here, my lord – a trifle of our love.
SECOND LORD
  With more than common thanks I will receive it.

---

182 *entertained* received   193 *Being of* (the desires of his heart) having
194 *state* means   197 *put . . . books* mortgaged to them   201 *such . . . exceed* such (friends) as do more harm than even his enemies   203 *bate . . . of*
reduce, undervalue

THIRD LORD
  O, he's the very soul of bounty!

TIMON   And now I remember, my lord, you gave good   207
  words the other day of a bay courser I rode on. 'Tis
  yours because you liked it.

FIRST LORD
  O, I beseech you pardon me, my lord, in that!   210

TIMON
  You may take my word, my lord, I know no man
  Can justly praise but what he does affect.   212
  I weigh my friends' affection with mine own.
  I'll tell you true; I'll call to you.   214

ALL LORDS   O none so welcome!

TIMON
  I take all and your several visitations   215
  So kind to heart 'tis not enough to give.
  Methinks I could deal kingdoms to my friends
  And ne'er be weary. Alcibiades,
  Thou art a soldier, therefore seldom rich.
  It comes in charity to thee; for all thy living   220
  Is 'mongst the dead, and all the lands thou hast
  Lie in a pitched field.   222

ALCIBIADES   Ay, defiled land, my lord.

FIRST LORD   We are so virtuously bound –

TIMON   And so
  Am I to you.

SECOND LORD   So infinitely endeared –

TIMON
  All to you. Lights, more lights!   225

207–8 *gave good words* spoke well   210 *pardon . . . that* i.e., don't ask me to
accept such a gift as that   212 *but* anything except; *affect* like   214 *call to*
call on (when in need)   215 *all . . . several* both your joint and separate
220 *It . . . thee* giving to you is real charity (since you have no property of
your own); *living* (1) life, (2) property   222 *defiled* (1) having, like a battle-
field, files of soldiers on it, (2) contaminated (since "he that toucheth pitch
shall be defiled with it," Ecclesiasticus 13 : 1)   225 *All to you* all the obligation is mine, to you

FIRST LORD   The best of happiness,
    Honor, and fortunes keep with you, Lord Timon!
TIMON
227   Ready for his friends.   *Exeunt Lords [and others.*
                        Manent Apemantus and Timon].
APEMANTUS   What a coil's here!
228   Serving of becks and jutting-out of bums!
229   I doubt whether their legs be worth the sums
230   That are given for 'em. Friendship's full of dregs.
    Methinks false hearts should never have sound legs.
    Thus honest fools lay out their wealth on curtsies.
TIMON
    Now, Apemantus, if thou wert not sullen,
    I would be good to thee.
APEMANTUS   No, I'll nothing; for if I should be bribed
    too, there would be none left to rail upon thee, and
237   then thou wouldst sin the faster. Thou giv'st so long,
    Timon, I fear me thou wilt give away thyself in paper
    shortly. What needs these feasts, pomps, and vainglo-
240   ries?
TIMON   Nay, an you begin to rail on society once, I am
    sworn not to give regard to you. Farewell, and come
    with better music.   *Exit.*
APEMANTUS   So. Thou wilt not hear me now; thou shalt
245   not then. I'll lock thy heaven from thee.
    O that men's ears should be
    To counsel deaf but not to flattery!   *Exit.*

                        *

---

227 s.d. *Manent* (they) remain; *coil* fuss   **228** *Serving of becks* bowing (and scraping)   **229** *legs* (1) limbs, (2) bows   **237–39** *Thou . . . shortly* you've so long been squandering your tangible assets that I fear you'll soon be giving away all that's left of yourself in such unreal property as promises, mere worthless notes   **245** *thy heaven* i.e., my good counsel

∾ **II.1** *Enter a Senator [with papers in his hand].*

SENATOR

  And late five thousand. To Varro and to Isidore   1
  He owes nine thousand, besides my former sum,
  Which makes it five-and-twenty. Still in motion   3
  Of raging waste! It cannot hold; it will not.
  If I want gold, steal but a beggar's dog   5
  And give it Timon – why, the dog coins gold.
  If I would sell my horse and buy twenty more
  Better than he – why, give my horse to Timon;
  Ask nothing, give it him – it foals me straight,   9
  And able horses. No porter at his gate,   10
  But rather one that smiles and still invites
  All that pass by. It cannot hold; no reason   12
  Can sound his state in safety. Caphis, ho!
  Caphis, I say!
    Enter Caphis.

CAPHIS   Here, sir. What is your pleasure?

SENATOR

  Get on your cloak and haste you to Lord Timon.
  Importune him for my moneys. Be not ceased   16
  With slight denial, nor then silenced when   17
  "Commend me to your master" and the cap
  Plays in the right hand, thus; but tell him
  My uses cry to me; I must serve my turn   20
  Out of mine own; his days and times are past,
  And my reliances on his fracted dates   22
  Have smit my credit. I love and honor him,   23
  But must not break my back to heal his finger.

II.1 The house of a senator of Athens   **1** *late* recently   **3–4** *Still . . . Of* constantly engaged in   **5** *steal but* I have only to steal   **9** *straight* straightaway **10** *able* good, strong   **12–13** *no . . . safety* no reasonable man can investigate his estate and find it financially secure   **16** *ceased* stopped   **17–19** *when . . . thus* when with . . . thus (he tries to put you off)   **20** *uses* needs   **22** *fracted* broken   **23** *smit* damaged

Immediate are my needs, and my relief
Must not be tossed and turned to me in words
But find supply immediate. Get you gone.
Put on a most importunate aspect,
A visage of demand; for I do fear,
30 When every feather sticks in his own wing,
31 Lord Timon will be left a naked gull,
32 Which flashes now a phoenix. Get you gone.

CAPHIS
I go, sir.
SENATOR   I go, sir? Take the bonds along with you
35 And have the dates in. Come.
CAPHIS   I will, sir.
SENATOR   Go.   *Exeunt.*

                          *

∽ **II.2** *Enter [Flavius, Timon's] Steward, with many bills
in his hand.*

STEWARD
No care, no stop; so senseless of expense
That he will neither know how to maintain it
Nor cease his flow of riot; takes no account
4 How things go from him nor resumes no care
5 Of what is to continue. Never mind
Was to be so unwise to be so kind.
7 What shall be done? He will not hear till feel.
8 I must be round with him, now he comes from hunting.
Fie, fie, fie, fie!

---

30 *every . . . wing* i.e., when all property is in the hands of its rightful owner
31 *gull* (1) unfledged bird, (2) dupe   32 *phoenix* (a gorgeous mythical bird,
a symbol of matchless beauty and immortality)   35 *dates in* due dates clearly
marked

   II.2 Before Timon's house   4 *resumes* takes   5 *what . . . continue* what
will serve future needs   5–6 *Never . . . kind* never was anyone so foolish as
to be so generous   7 *hear till feel* listen until he feels the consequences of his
extravagance   8 *round* blunt

Enter Caphis [and the Servants of] Isidore and Varro.

CAPHIS

Good even, Varro. What, you come for money?   10

VARRO'S SERVANT

Is't not your business too?

CAPHIS

It is; and yours too, Isidore?

ISIDORE'S SERVANT   It is so.

CAPHIS

Would we were all discharged!   13

VARRO'S SERVANT   I fear it.

CAPHIS

Here comes the lord.

Enter Timon and his train [with Alcibiades].

TIMON

So soon as dinner's done we'll forth again,

My Alcibiades. – With me? What is your will?

CAPHIS

My lord, here is a note of certain dues.

TIMON

Dues? Whence are you?

CAPHIS   Of Athens here, my lord.

TIMON

Go to my steward.

CAPHIS

Please it your lordship, he hath put me off   20

To the succession of new days this month.   21

My master is awaked by great occasion   22

To call upon his own, and humbly prays you   23

That with your other noble parts you'll suit   24

In giving him his right.

---

13 *it* i.e., that we won't be   21 *To . . . days* i.e., from one day to the next   22
awaked . . . occasion aroused by serious need   23 *call . . . own* call in what is
owed him (so that he may pay his debts)   24 *suit* be consistent

TIMON   Mine honest friend,
26   I prithee but repair to me next morning.
CAPHIS
    Nay, good my lord –
TIMON   Contain thyself, good friend.
VARRO'S SERVANT
    One Varro's servant, my good lord –
ISIDORE'S SERVANT
    From Isidore; he humbly prays your speedy payment.
CAPHIS
30   If you did know, my lord, my master's wants –
VARRO'S SERVANT
31   'Twas due on forfeiture, my lord, six weeks and past.
ISIDORE'S SERVANT
    Your steward puts me off, my lord, and I
    Am sent expressly to your lordship.
TIMON
    Give me breath.
35   I do beseech you, good my lords, keep on;
    I'll wait upon you instantly.
                              [Exeunt Alcibiades, Lords, etc.]
        [To Flavius]   Come hither. Pray you,
37   How goes the world that I am thus encountered
    With clamorous demands of debt, broken bonds,
39   And the detention of long-since-due debts,
40   Against my honor?
STEWARD   Please you, gentlemen,
    The time is unagreeable to this business.
    Your importunacy cease till after dinner,
    That I may make his lordship understand
    Wherefore you are not paid.

---

26 *repair* return 31 *on forfeiture* under penalty of forfeit if not paid 35–36
keep on . . . instantly go ahead (without me); I'll be with you again in no time
37 *goes the world* can it be 39 *the detention* withholding payment 40
Against my honor thus calling my honor into question

TIMON

Do so, my friends – See them well entertained. *[Exit.]*

STEWARD

Pray draw near.   *Exit.* 46

Enter Apemantus and Fool.

CAPHIS

Stay, stay; here comes the fool with Apemantus.

Let's ha' some sport with 'em.

VARRO'S SERVANT   Hang him, he'll abuse us.

ISIDORE'S SERVANT   A plague upon him, dog!   50

VARRO'S SERVANT   How dost, fool?

APEMANTUS   Dost dialogue with thy shadow?

VARRO'S SERVANT   I speak not to thee.

APEMANTUS   No, 'tis to thyself. *[To the Fool]* Come
away.

ISIDORE'S SERVANT   *[To Varro's Servant]* There's the fool
hangs on your back already.   57

APEMANTUS   No, thou stand'st single; thou'rt not on him   58
yet.

CAPHIS   Where's the fool now?   60

APEMANTUS   He last asked the question. Poor rogues and
usurers' men; bawds between gold and want!   62

ALL SERVANTS   What are we, Apemantus?

APEMANTUS   Asses.

ALL SERVANTS   Why?

APEMANTUS   That you ask me what you are, and do not
know yourselves. Speak to 'em, fool.

FOOL   How do you, gentlemen?

ALL SERVANTS   Gramercies, good fool. How does your   69
mistress?   70

---

46 *draw near* come this way   57 *hangs . . . back* (a fool sign has already been
hung on you; you've already been associated with the fool) 58–59
thou'rt . . . yet you haven't yet been identified with *him* (Isidore's servant)   62
bawds procurers or middlemen who connect usurers and those in need   69
Gramercies many thanks

FOOL   She's e'en setting on water to scald such chickens
72   as you are. Would we could see you at Corinth!

APEMANTUS   Good! Gramercy.

Enter Page.

FOOL   Look you, here comes my mistress' page.

PAGE   *[To the Fool]* Why, how now, captain? What do
    you in this wise company? How dost thou, Apemantus?

APEMANTUS   Would I had a rod in my mouth, that I
78   might answer thee profitably.

79   PAGE   Prithee, Apemantus, read me the superscription of
80   these letters; I know not which is which.

APEMANTUS   Canst not read?

PAGE   No.

APEMANTUS   There will little learning die then that day
    thou art hanged. This is to Lord Timon, this to Alcibi-
    ades. Go; thou wast born a bastard and thou'lt die a
    bawd.

87   PAGE   Thou wast whelped a dog and thou shalt famish a
    dog's death. Answer not; I am gone.   *Exit.*

89   APEMANTUS   E'en so thou outrun'st grace. Fool, I will go
90   with you to Lord Timon's.

FOOL   Will you leave me there?

92   APEMANTUS   If Timon stay at home – You three serve
    three usurers?

ALL SERVANTS   Ay. Would they served us!

APEMANTUS   So would I – as good a trick as ever hang-
    man served thief.

FOOL   Are you three usurers' men?

ALL SERVANTS   Ay, fool.

FOOL   I think no usurer but has a fool to his servant. My
100   mistress is one, and I am her fool. When men come to

---

72 *Corinth* (a city notorious for its brothels)   **78** *answer . . . profitably* make
my answer to you a chastisement (or beating) that would profit you   **79** *superscription* address   **87** *famish* starve (which is *a dog's death*)   **89** *grace*
i.e., the blessing of being chastised by me   **92** *If . . . home* i.e., as long as
Timon is there, a fool will be present

borrow of your masters, they approach sadly and go
away merry; but they enter my mistress' house merrily
and go away sadly. The reason of this?

VARRO'S SERVANT   I could render one.   104

APEMANTUS   Do it then, that we may account thee a
whoremaster and a knave; which notwithstanding,
thou shalt be no less esteemed.

VARRO'S SERVANT   What is a whoremaster, fool?

FOOL   A fool in good clothes, and something like thee.
'Tis a spirit; sometime't appears like a lord, sometime   110
like a lawyer, sometime like a philosopher, with two
stones more than's artificial one. He is very often like a   112
knight; and, generally, in all shapes that man goes up
and down in, from fourscore to thirteen, this spirit
walks in.

VARRO'S SERVANT   Thou art not altogether a fool.

FOOL   Nor thou altogether a wise man. As much foolery
as I have, so much wit thou lack'st.

APEMANTUS   That answer might have become Ape-
mantus.   120

ALL SERVANTS   Aside, aside; here comes Lord Timon.
   Enter Timon and [Flavius, his] Steward.

APEMANTUS   Come with me, fool, come.

FOOL   I do not always follow lover, elder brother, and   123
woman; sometime the philosopher.
                              [Exeunt Apemantus and Fool.]

STEWARD
Pray you, walk near; I'll speak with you anon.
                                      Exeunt [Servants].

TIMON
You make me marvel wherefore ere this time

---

104 *one* (for instance that they are now poorer – and probably diseased as
well – from having paid to have sex with infected prostitutes)   112 *stones*
testicles; *artificial one* i.e., the philosophers' stone, which was thought to
transform base metals into gold   123–24 *lover . . . woman* i.e., people likely,
for one reason or another, to prove generous

127   Had you not fully laid my state before me,
128   That I might so have rated my expense
       As I had leave of means.

STEWARD   You would not hear me;
130   At many leisures I proposed –

TIMON   Go to!
131   Perchance some single vantages you took,
       When my indisposition put you back,
133   And that unaptness made your minister
       Thus to excuse yourself.

STEWARD   O my good lord,
       At many times I brought in my accounts,
       Laid them before you. You would throw them off
137   And say you found them in mine honesty.
       When for some trifling present you have bid me
       Return so much, I have shook my head and wept;
140   Yea, 'gainst th' authority of manners prayed you
       To hold your hand more close. I did endure
142   Not seldom, nor no slight checks, when I have
143   Prompted you in the ebb of your estate
       And your great flow of debts. My lovèd lord,
145   Though you hear now too late, yet now's a time:
146   The greatest of your having lacks a half
       To pay your present debts.

TIMON   Let all my land be sold.

STEWARD
148   'Tis all engaged, some forfeited and gone;
       And what remains will hardly stop the mouth

---

127 *state* financial position   128–29 *rated . . . means* adjusted my expenditures as I had access to or control over wealth   131 *vantages* opportunities   133–34 *And . . . excuse yourself* and made that indisposition serve you as an excuse thereafter   137 *found . . . honesty* had all the information you wanted in knowing me to be honest   142 *seldom* infrequent (an adjective, modifying *checks*)   143 *Prompted . . . in* called your attention to   145 *now's a time* i.e., better late than never   146–47 *The greatest . . . debts* what you own won't, at best, pay half what you owe   148 *engaged* mortgaged

Of present dues. The future comes apace;   150
What shall defend the interim? and at length   151
How goes our reck'ning?

TIMON
To Lacedaemon did my land extend.   153

STEWARD
O my good lord, the world is but a word;   154
Were it all yours to give it in a breath,
How quickly were it gone!

TIMON   You tell me true.

STEWARD
If you suspect my husbandry of falsehood,   157
Call me before th' exactest auditors
And set me on the proof. So the gods bless me,   159
When all our offices have been oppressed   160
With riotous feeders, when our vaults have wept
With drunken spilth of wine, when every room   162
Hath blazed with lights and brayed with minstrelsy,
I have retired me to a wasteful cock   164
And set mine eyes at flow.   165

TIMON   Prithee no more.

STEWARD
Heavens, have I said, the bounty of this lord!
How many prodigal bits have slaves and peasants   167
This night englutted! Who is not Timon's?   168
What heart, head, sword, force, means, but is Lord
    Timon's?
Great Timon; noble, worthy, royal Timon!   170
Ah, when the means are gone that buy this praise,

---

150 *present dues* immediate obligations 151–52 *What . . . reck'ning* what
shall we meanwhile use to ward off disaster, and what will our eventual fate
be 153 *Lacedaemon* Sparta 154 *world . . . word* (the two words were pronounced similarly in Elizabethan English) 157 *husbandry* household man-
agement 159 *set me on* put me to 160 *offices* kitchens, pantries, etc. 162
spilth spilling 164 *wasteful cock* leaky tap (of a wine barrel) 165 *set . . .
flow* wept 167 *prodigal bits* lavish morsels 168 *englutted* swallowed; *is not*
does not profess to be

The breath is gone whereof this praise is made.
173   Feast-won, fast-lost: one cloud of winter show'rs,
174   These flies are couched.
TIMON   Come, sermon me no further.
No villainous bounty yet hath passed my heart;
Unwisely, not ignobly, have I given.
177   Why, dost thou weep? Canst thou the conscience lack
178   To think I shall lack friends? Secure thy heart;
If I would broach the vessels of my love
180   And try the argument of hearts by borrowing,
Men and men's fortunes could I frankly use
182   As I can bid thee speak.
STEWARD   Assurance bless your thoughts!
TIMON
And in some sort these wants of mine are crowned,
184   That I account them blessings; for by these
Shall I try friends. You shall perceive how you
Mistake my fortunes; I am wealthy in my friends.
Within there! Flaminius! Servilius!
      *Enter three Servants [Flaminius, Servilius, and
      another].*
SERVANTS   My lord? My lord?
TIMON   I will dispatch you severally – *[To Servilius]* you
190   to Lord Lucius; *[To Flaminius]* to Lord Lucullus you; I
hunted with his honor today; *[To the other]* you to
Sempronius. Commend me to their loves; and I am
proud, say, that my occasions have found time to use
194   'em toward a supply of money. Let the request be fifty
talents.
FLAMINIUS   As you have said, my lord. *[Exeunt Servants.]*
STEWARD   *[Aside]* Lord Lucius and Lucullus? Humh.

---

173 *Feast-won, fast-lost* (those friends Timon won through generosity will
flee now that his resources have been exhausted)   174 *couched* gone into
hiding   177 *conscience* judgment   178 *Secure* set at ease   180 *try the argument* test the protestations   182 *Assurance . . . thoughts* may it prove so   184
That so that   194–201 *fifty . . . A thousand talents* (large sums indeed: see
I.1.95n.)

TIMON
  Go you, sir, to the senators,
  Of whom, even to the state's best health, I have   199
  Deserved this hearing. Bid 'em send o' th' instant   200
  A thousand talents to me.
STEWARD   I have been bold,
  For that I knew it the most general way,   202
  To them to use your signet and your name;   203
  But they do shake their heads, and I am here
  No richer in return.
TIMON   Is't true? Can 't be?
STEWARD
  They answer in a joint and corporate voice
  That now they are at fall, want treasure, cannot   207
  Do what they would, are sorry: you are honorable,
  But yet they could have wished – they know not –
  Something hath been amiss – a noble nature   210
  May catch a wrench – would all were well – 'tis pity –   211
  And so, intending other serious matters,   212
  After distasteful looks and these hard fractions,   213
  With certain half-caps and cold-moving nods   214
  They froze me into silence.
TIMON   You gods, reward them!
  Prithee, man, look cheerly. These old fellows
  Have their ingratitude in them hereditary.
  Their blood is caked, 'tis cold, it seldom flows;
  'Tis lack of kindly warmth they are not kind;   219
  And nature, as it grows again toward earth,   220
  Is fashioned for the journey, dull and heavy.
  Go to Ventidius. Prithee be not sad;

---

199 *even . . . health* the very soundness of the state's treasury being due to me
202 *general* usual   203 *signet* ring used as a seal and as a symbol of authorization   207 *fall* low ebb; *want treasure* lack funds   211 *catch a wrench* suffer a reverse   212 *intending* pretending, busying themselves with   213 *hard
fractions* unfeeling fragments of sentences   214 *half-caps* half-hearted saluta-
tions   219 *lack* i.e., from lack; *kindly* (1) natural, (2) generous   220
grows . . . earth nears the grave

223   Thou art true and honest; ingeniously I speak,
      No blame belongs to thee. Ventidius lately
      Buried his father, by whose death he's stepped
      Into a great estate. When he was poor,
      Imprisoned, and in scarcity of friends,
228   I cleared him with five talents. Greet him from me.
229   Bid him suppose some good necessity
230   Touches his friend, which craves to be remembered
      With those five talents. That had, give't these fellows
      To whom 'tis instant due. Ne'er speak or think
      That Timon's fortunes 'mong his friends can sink.

STEWARD
      I would I could not think it.
235   That thought is bounty's foe;
236   Being free itself, it thinks all others so.   *Exeunt.*

                              *

∾ **III.1** *Flaminius waiting to speak with a Lord, [Lucul-
      lus,] from his Master; enters a Servant to him.*

SERVANT   I have told my lord of you; he is coming down
      to you.
FLAMINIUS   I thank you, sir.
      Enter Lucullus.
SERVANT   Here's my lord.
LUCULLUS   *[Aside]* One of Lord Timon's men? A gift, I
6   warrant. Why, this hits right; I dreamt of a silver basin
      and ewer tonight. – Flaminius, honest Flaminius, you
8   are very respectively welcome, sir. Fill me some wine.

---

223 *ingeniously* sincerely   228 *cleared* canceled his debts, freed   229 *good*
genuine   230–31 *craves . . . talents* i.e., asks that Ventidius recall the gift that
restored his freedom – and reciprocate   235–36 *That thought . . . so* (ob-
scure, metrically odd; perhaps the thought that Timon's friends could desert
him undermines generosity)   236 *free* generous

III.1 The house of Lucullus   6 *hits right* is just as it should be   8 *respectively* particularly

[Exit Servant.] And how does that honorable, complete, freehearted gentleman of Athens, thy very bountiful good lord and master? 10

FLAMINIUS   His health is well, sir.

LUCULLUS   I am right glad that his health is well, sir. And what hast thou there under thy cloak, pretty Flaminius?

FLAMINIUS   Faith, nothing but an empty box, sir, which in my lord's behalf I come to entreat your honor to supply; 16 who, having great and instant occasion to use fifty talents, hath sent to your lordship to furnish him, nothing doubting your present assistance therein.

LUCULLUS   La, la, la, la! "Nothing doubting," says he? 20 Alas, good lord! a noble gentleman 'tis, if he would not keep so good a house. Many a time and often I ha' 22 dined with him and told him on't, and come again to supper to him of purpose to have him spend less; and yet he would embrace no counsel, take no warning by my coming. Every man has his fault, and honesty is his. 26 I ha' told him on't, but I could ne'er get him from't.

Enter Servant with wine.

SERVANT   Please your lordship, here is the wine.

LUCULLUS   Flaminius, I have noted thee always wise. Here's to thee. 30

FLAMINIUS   Your lordship speaks your pleasure. 31

LUCULLUS   I have observed thee always for a towardly 32 prompt spirit, give thee thy due, and one that knows what belongs to reason, and canst use the time well if the time use thee well. Good parts in thee! *[To Servant]* 35 Get you gone, sirrah. *[Exit Servant.]* Draw nearer, honest Flaminius. Thy lord's a bountiful gentleman; but thou art wise, and thou know'st well enough, although

---

16–17 *supply* fill   **22** *keep ... house* be so hospitable   **26** *honesty* generosity
30 *Here's to thee* (drinking the wine originally meant for Flaminius)   **31** *speaks your pleasure* is pleased to say so   **32–33** *towardly prompt* friendly and well-disposed   **35** *parts* qualities

thou com'st to me, that this is no time to lend money,
40   especially upon bare friendship without security. Here's
41   three solidares for thee. Good boy, wink at me and say
thou saw'st me not. Fare thee well.

FLAMINIUS

43   Is't possible the world should so much differ,
And we alive that lived? Fly, damnèd baseness,
To him that worships thee!
        [Throws the money back.]

LUCULLUS   Ha! Now I see thou art a fool, and fit for thy
        master.   Exit Lucullus.

FLAMINIUS

48   May these add to the number that may scald thee!
Let molten coin be thy damnation,
50   Thou disease of a friend, and not himself!
Has friendship such a faint and milky heart
It turns in less than two nights? O you gods,
53   I feel my master's passion. This slave unto his honor
Has my lord's meat in him.
Why should it thrive and turn to nutriment
When he is turned to poison?
O may diseases only work upon't;
58   And when he's sick to death, let not that part of nature
Which my lord paid for be of any power
60   To expel sickness, but prolong his hour!   Exit.

                        *

～ III.2 *Enter Lucius with three Strangers.*

LUCIUS   Who? the Lord Timon? He is my very good
    friend and an honorable gentleman.

_____

41 *solidares* (of Shakespeare's invention but evidently for coins of no great
worth) 43–44 *Is't . . . lived* can we possibly have lived long enough to see
the world so much changed 48–49 *May . . . damnation* may you burn for
your greed, may you choke on this 53 *passion* anger (?), suffering (?) 58 *of
nature* i.e., of his body 60 *hour* time of suffering
    III.2 A public place in Athens

FIRST STRANGER We know him for no less, though we
are but strangers to him. But I can tell you one thing,
my lord, and which I hear from common rumors: now
Lord Timon's happy hours are done and past, and his
estate shrinks from him.

LUCIUS   Fie, no, do not believe it; he cannot want for
money.

SECOND STRANGER But believe you this, my lord, that   10
not long ago one of his men was with the Lord Lucullus to borrow so many talents; nay, urged extremely   12
for't, and showed what necessity belonged to't, and yet
was denied.

LUCIUS   How?

SECOND STRANGER   I tell you denied, my lord.

LUCIUS   What a strange case was that! Now before the
gods, I am ashamed on't. Denied that honorable man?
There was very little honor showed in't. For my own
part, I must needs confess, I have received some small   20
kindnesses from him, as money, plate, jewels, and such-
like trifles – nothing comparing to his; yet had he mis-   22
took him and sent to me, I should ne'er have denied his   23
occasion so many talents.

Enter Servilius.

SERVILIUS   See, by good hap, yonder's my lord. I have   25
sweat to see his honor. – My honored lord!   26

LUCIUS   Servilius? You are kindly met, sir. Fare thee well;
commend me to thy honorable virtuous lord, my very
exquisite friend.

SERVILIUS   May it please your honor, my lord hath sent –   30

LUCIUS   Ha! What has he sent? I am so much endeared
to that lord! He's ever sending. How shall I thank him,
think'st thou? And what has he sent now?

12, 24 *so many* (possibly expressions that the author intended to change later
to specific numbers) 22–23 *mistook . . . me* made the mistake of sending to
me, a man who owed him less 23–24 *denied his occasion* refused him in his
need 25 *hap* luck 26 *sweat* rushed or been anxious

34 SERVILIUS Has only sent his present occasion now, my
       lord, requesting your lordship to supply his instant use
36   with so many talents.
     LUCIUS
       I know his lordship is but merry with me;
38   He cannot want fifty – five hundred – talents.
     SERVILIUS
       But in the meantime he wants less, my lord.
40   If his occasion were not virtuous,
       I should not urge it half so faithfully.
     LUCIUS
       Dost thou speak seriously, Servilius?
     SERVILIUS
       Upon my soul, 'tis true, sir.
44 LUCIUS What a wicked beast was I to disfurnish myself
45   against such a good time, when I might ha' shown my-
       self honorable! How unluckily it happened that I
47   should purchase the day before for a little part and
       undo a great deal of honor! Servilius, now before the
       gods, I am not able to do – the more beast, I say – I was
50   sending to use Lord Timon myself, these gentlemen
       can witness; but I would not for the wealth of Athens I
       had done't now. Commend me bountifully to his good
       lordship; and I hope his honor will conceive the fairest
       of me, because I have no power to be kind. And tell
       him this from me: I count it one of my greatest afflic-
       tions, say, that I cannot pleasure such an honorable
       gentleman. Good Servilius, will you befriend me so far
       as to use mine own words to him?
     SERVILIUS Yes, sir, I shall.

---

34 *Has* he has; *his present occasion* word of his urgent need 36 *so many* (see
III.2.12n.) 38 *fifty – five hundred* (perhaps indicating the author's uncer-
tainty as to which number he should use) 44 *disfurnish* leave unprepared
45 *against... time* for dealing with such an opportunity 47–48 *for...*
honor a trifling business interest, and thereby lose the chance of gaining
great honor by helping Timon 50 *use* i.e., borrow from

LUCIUS
    I'll look you out a good turn, Servilius.   *Exit Servilius.* 60
    True, as you said, Timon is shrunk indeed;
    And he that's once denied will hardly speed.   *Exit.* 62
FIRST STRANGER
    Do you observe this, Hostilius?
SECOND STRANGER   Ay, too well.
FIRST STRANGER
    Why, this is the world's soul, and just of the same piece 64
    Is every flatterer's sport. Who can call him 65
    His friend that dips in the same dish? For in
    My knowing Timon has been this lord's father 67
    And kept his credit with his purse,
    Supported his estate. Nay, Timon's money
    Has paid his men their wages. He ne'er drinks 70
    But Timon's silver treads upon his lip;
    And yet – O, see the monstrousness of man
    When he looks out in an ungrateful shape! – 73
    He does deny him, in respect of his, 74
    What charitable men afford to beggars.
THIRD STRANGER
    Religion groans at it.
FIRST STRANGER   For mine own part,
    I never tasted Timon in my life, 77
    Nor came any of his bounties over me
    To mark me for his friend; yet I protest,
    For his right noble mind, illustrious virtue, 80
    And honorable carriage, 81
    Had his necessity made use of me,
    I would have put my wealth into donation 83

---

60 *look you out* find a way to do you 62 *speed* prosper 64 *world's soul* essence of this corrupt world 65 *sport* entertainment 67 *father* sponsor, protector 73 *looks out in* shows himself as 74–75 *in respect . . . afford* considering his wealth, even the pittance good men give 77 *tasted Timon* i.e., sampled his liberality 81 *carriage* conduct 83 *put . . . donation* treated my wealth as a gift from Timon

And the best half should have returned to him,
So much I love his heart. But I perceive
Men must learn now with pity to dispense;
87   For policy sits above conscience.   *Exeunt.*

*

∾ **III.3** *Enter a third Servant [of Timon's] with Sempronius, another of Timon's Friends.*

SEMPRONIUS
    Must he needs trouble me in't – hum! – 'bove all others?
    He might have tried Lord Lucius or Lucullus;
    And now Ventidius is wealthy too,
    Whom he redeemed from prison. All these
    Owes their estates unto him.
SERVANT   My lord,
6   They have all been touched and found base metal,
7   For they have all denied him.
SEMPRONIUS   How? Have they denied him?
    Has Ventidius and Lucullus denied him,
9   And does he send to me? Three? Humh!
10   It shows but little love or judgment in him.
    Must I be his last refuge? His friends, like physicians,
12   Thrive, give him over. Must I take th' cure upon me?
13   Has much disgraced me in't; I'm angry at him,
14   That might have known my place. I see no sense for't
    But his occasions might have wooed me first;
16   For, in my conscience, I was the first man
    That e'er received gift from him;
    And does he think so backwardly of me now
    That I'll requite it last? No.

---

87 *policy* self-interested strategy
    III.3 The house of Sempronius   6 *touched* tested (as with a touchstone)
7 *denied* refused   9 *Three* (Lucius as well as Ventidius and Lucullus)   12
Thrive . . . over profit from him, then give up on him   13 *Has* he has   14
place (i.e., ahead of Lucius, Lucullus, and Ventidius)   16 *in my conscience* to
my knowledge

So it may prove an argument of laughter   20
To th' rest, and I 'mongst lords be thought a fool.
I'd rather than the worth of thrice the sum
Had sent to me first, but for my mind's sake;   23
I'd such a courage to do him good. But now return,   24
And with their faint reply this answer join:
Who bates mine honor shall not know my coin. *Exit.*   26
SERVANT   Excellent! Your lordship's a goodly villain. The
devil knew not what he did when he made man politic.
He crossed himself by't; and I cannot think but in the   29
end the villainies of man will set him clear. How fairly   30
this lord strives to appear foul! takes virtuous copies to   31
be wicked, like those that under hot ardent zeal would   32
set whole realms on fire. Of such a nature is his politic
love.
This was my lord's best hope; now all are fled
Save only the gods. Now his friends are dead.
Doors that were ne'er acquainted with their wards   37
Many a bounteous year must be employed
Now to guard sure their master.   39
And this is all a liberal course allows: 40
Who cannot keep his wealth must keep his house.   41
                                                        Exit.

*

---

20 *argument of* subject for   **23** *Had* he had   **24** *courage* inclination   **26**
bates detracts from   **29** *crossed* thwarted (since man thus becomes his superior in evil)   **30** *set him clear* make the devil look innocent   **31–32** *takes . . .
wicked* studies virtue, but only in the interests of wickedness   **32–33** *like . . .
fire* like those who justify warfare, treason, or terrorism (perhaps an allusion
to the Gunpowder Plot, a Catholic conspiracy to blow up Parliament on its
opening day, thus killing King James I, his wife, and male heirs, and most of
the powerful men in the kingdom; the conspirators' *ardent zeal* for a
Catholic monarch supposedly motivated them)   **37** *wards* locks   **39** *guard
sure* (lest he be arrested for debt)   **41** *keep . . . keep* preserve . . . stay inside

∾ **III.4** *Enter [two of] Varro's [Men], meeting [Lucius'*
Servant and] others, all [being servants of] Timon's
creditors, to wait for his coming out. Then enter
[Titus] and Hortensius.

FIRST VARRO'S MAN
 Well met; good morrow, Titus and Hortensius.
TITUS
 The like to you, kind Varro.
HORTENSIUS   Lucius!
 What, do we meet together?
LUCIUS' SERVANT   Ay, and I think
 One business does command us all, for mine
 Is money.
TITUS
 So is theirs and ours.
  Enter Philotus.
LUCIUS' SERVANT   And Sir Philotus too!
PHILOTUS
7 Good day at once.
LUCIUS' SERVANT   Welcome, good brother.
8 What do you think the hour?
PHILOTUS   Laboring for nine.
LUCIUS' SERVANT
 So much?
PHILOTUS Is not my lord seen yet?
LUCIUS' SERVANT   Not yet.
PHILOTUS
10 I wonder on't; he was wont to shine at seven.
LUCIUS' SERVANT
11 Ay, but the days are waxed shorter with him.
 You must consider that a prodigal course
 Is like the sun's,

III.4 The house of Timon 7 *at once* to all of you 8 *Laboring for* slowly approaching 11 *waxed* become (not here, as often, "grown larger")

But not, like his, recoverable. I fear   14
'Tis deepest winter in Lord Timon's purse;
That is, one may reach deep enough and yet   16
Find little.

PHILOTUS   I am of your fear for that.

TITUS
I'll show you how t' observe a strange event.
Your lord sends now for money.

HORTENSIUS   Most true, he does.

TITUS
And he wears jewels now of Timon's gift,   20
For which I wait for money.   21

HORTENSIUS
It is against my heart.

LUCIUS' SERVANT   Mark how strange it shows:
Timon in this should pay more than he owes,
And e'en as if your lord should wear rich jewels   24
And send for money for 'em.

HORTENSIUS
I'm weary of this charge, the gods can witness;
I know my lord hath spent of Timon's wealth,
And now ingratitude makes it worse than stealth.   28

FIRST VARRO'S MAN
Yes, mine's three thousand crowns; what's yours?

LUCIUS' SERVANT
Five thousand mine.   30

FIRST VARRO'S MAN
'Tis much deep; and it should seem by th' sum   31
Your master's confidence was above mine,   32
Else surely his had equaled.   33

    Enter Flaminius.

---

14 *recoverable* retraceable (with quibble on idea of financial recovery) **16**
reach deep enough (as do animals digging deep in the snow for food) **21**
For . . . money for buying which Timon borrowed the money I now seek
from him **24–25** *wear . . . 'em* not only wear the rich jewels given him but
also ask for the money that bought them **28** *stealth* theft **31** *much* very
32 *above mine* greater than my master's **33** *his* my master's loan

TITUS   One of Lord Timon's men.
LUCIUS' SERVANT   Flaminius? Sir, a word. Pray, is my lord
   ready to come forth?
FLAMINIUS   No, indeed he is not.
TITUS   We attend his lordship; pray signify so much.
FLAMINIUS   I need not tell him that; he knows you are
40   too diligent.   [Exit.]
      Enter [Timon's] Steward, [Flavius,] in a cloak,
      muffled.
LUCIUS' SERVANT
   Ha, is not that his steward muffled so?
42   He goes away in a cloud. Call him, call him!
TITUS   Do you hear, sir?
SECOND VARRO'S MAN   By your leave, sir –
STEWARD
   What do ye ask of me, my friend?
TITUS
   We wait for certain money here, sir.
STEWARD   Ay,
   If money were as certain as your waiting,
   'Twere sure enough.
49   Why then preferred you not your sums and bills
50   When your false masters ate of my lord's meat?
   Then they could smile, and fawn upon his debts,
52   And take down th' int'rest into their glutt'nous maws.
   You do yourselves but wrong to stir me up;
   Let me pass quietly.
   Believe't, my lord and I have made an end;
   I have no more to reckon, he to spend.
LUCIUS' SERVANT
   Ay, but this answer will not serve.

---

42 *in a cloud* (1) disguised, (2) gloomily   49 *preferred* presented   52 *th' in-
t'rest* i.e., the food Timon provided was one kind of interest they got on their
loans

STEWARD

   If 'twill not serve, 'tis not so base as you,

   For you serve knaves.   *[Exit.]*

FIRST VARRO'S MAN   How? What does his cashiered wor- 60
ship mutter?

SECOND VARRO'S MAN   No matter what; he's poor, and
that's revenge enough. Who can speak broader than he 63
that has no house to put his head in? Such may rail
against great buildings.

   Enter Servilius.

TITUS   O, here's Servilius; now we shall know some answer.

SERVILIUS   If I might beseech you, gentlemen, to repair 68
some other hour, I should derive much from't. For
take't of my soul, my lord leans wondrously to discon- 70
tent. His comfortable temper has forsook him; he's
much out of health and keeps his chamber.

LUCIUS' SERVANT

   Many do keep their chambers are not sick;   73

   And if it be so far beyond his health,   74

   Methinks he should the sooner pay his debts

   And make a clear way to the gods.   76

SERVILIUS   Good gods!

TITUS

   We cannot take this for answer, sir.

FLAMINIUS   *Within*

   Servilius, help! My lord, my lord!

   Enter Timon, in a rage.

TIMON

   What, are my doors opposed against my passage?

   Have I been ever free, and must my house   80

---

60 *cashiered* dismissed 63 *broader* more freely (with quibble on idea of
being abroad) 68 *repair* come back 73 *are* who are 74 *it be . . . health* his
state is so unhealthy 76 *And . . . to the gods* and clear his path to heaven
80 *free* (1) at liberty, (2) generous

Be my retentive enemy, my jail?
The place which I have feasted, does it now,
Like all mankind, show me an iron heart?

84 LUCIUS' SERVANT   Put in now, Titus.

TITUS   My lord, here is my bill.

LUCIUS' SERVANT   Here's mine.

HORTENSIUS   And mine, my lord.

BOTH VARRO'S MEN   And ours, my lord.

PHILOTUS   All our bills.

TIMON

90   Knock me down with 'em; cleave me to the girdle!

LUCIUS' SERVANT   Alas, my lord –

TIMON   Cut my heart in sums!

TITUS   Mine, fifty talents.

94 TIMON   Tell out my blood!

LUCIUS' SERVANT   Five thousand crowns, my lord.

TIMON   Five thousand drops pays that. What yours? and
yours?

FIRST VARRO'S MAN   My lord –

SECOND VARRO'S MAN   My lord –

100 TIMON   Tear me, take me, and the gods fall upon you!

Exit.

101 HORTENSIUS   Faith, I perceive our masters may throw
their caps at their money. These debts may well be
called desperate ones, for a madman owes 'em. *Exeunt.*
Enter Timon [and Flavius, his Steward].

TIMON   They have e'en put my breath from me, the
slaves! Creditors? Devils!

STEWARD   My dear lord –

107 TIMON   What if it should be so?

STEWARD   My lord –

TIMON   I'll have it so. My steward!

---

84 *Put in* make your claim   90 *Knock ... girdle* (since *bills* also meant
weapons that could split a man to his belt)   94 *Tell out* count out drops of
101–102 *throw ... at* give up hoping for   107 *What ... so* I wonder if it
would work (Timon has just thought of giving his mock banquet: see ll.
111–13; also III.6)

STEWARD   Here, my lord.   *110*

TIMON
  So fitly? Go, bid all my friends again,   *111*
  Lucius, Lucullus, and Sempronius – all.
  I'll once more feast the rascals.

STEWARD   O my lord,
  You only speak from your distracted soul;
  There's not so much left to furnish out   *115*
  A moderate table.

TIMON   Be it not in thy care. Go,
  I charge thee, invite them all; let in the tide
  Of knaves once more; my cook and I'll provide.

                                    Exeunt.

*

❧ **III.5** *Enter three Senators at one door, Alcibiades*
    meeting them, with Attendants.

FIRST SENATOR
  My lord, you have my voice to't; the fault's   *1*
  Bloody; 'tis necessary he should die.
  Nothing emboldens sin so much as mercy.

SECOND SENATOR
  Most true. The law shall bruise 'em.

ALCIBIADES
  Honor, health, and compassion to the Senate!

FIRST SENATOR
  Now, captain?

ALCIBIADES
  I am an humble suitor to your virtues;
  For pity is the virtue of the law,   *8*
  And none but tyrants use it cruelly.
  It pleases time and fortune to lie heavy   *10*

---

111 *fitly* opportunely   115 *to* as to
  III.5 The Senate House   1 *my voice to't* my vote for it (the death sentence
we are considering)   8 *virtue* defining characteristic, essence

Upon a friend of mine, who in hot blood
12 Hath stepped into the law, which is past depth
To those that without heed do plunge into't.
He is a man, setting his fate aside,
Of comely virtues;
16 Nor did he soil the fact with cowardice
(An honor in him which buys out his fault)
But with a noble fury and fair spirit,
19 Seeing his reputation touched to death,
20 He did oppose his foe;
21 And with such sober and unnoted passion
22 He did behove his anger, ere 'twas spent,
As if he had but proved an argument.

FIRST SENATOR
24 You undergo too strict a paradox,
Striving to make an ugly deed look fair.
Your words have took such pains as if they labored
27 To bring manslaughter into form and set
28 Quarreling upon the head of valor; which indeed
Is valor misbegot, and came into the world
30 When sects and factions were newly born.
He's truly valiant that can wisely suffer
The worst that man can breathe, and make his wrongs
33 His outsides, to wear them like his raiment, carelessly,
34 And ne'er prefer his injuries to his heart,
To bring it into danger.
36 If wrongs be evils, and enforce us kill,
What folly 'tis to hazard life for ill!

---

12 *stepped into* i.e., to some extent violated; *past depth* overwhelming   16
soil the fact blemish his deed   19 *touched to death* fatally threatened   21
sober and unnoted moderate and unremarkable   22 *behove* make use of   24
undergo . . . paradox are trying to maintain too highly strained an argument
27 *bring . . . into form* authorize   27–28 *set . . . head* make dueling the
highest manifestation   28 *Quarreling . . . which* i.e., fighting duels   33 *His
outsides* mere externals, nothing vital to him   34 *prefer* present   36 *and . . .
kill* and force us to avenge them

ALCIBIADES
  My lord –   38
FIRST SENATOR   You cannot make gross sins look clear.
  To revenge is no valor, but to bear.   39
ALCIBIADES
  My lords, then, under favor, pardon me   40
  If I speak like a captain.
  Why do fond men expose themselves to battle   42
  And not endure all threats? sleep upon't,   43
  And let the foes quietly cut their throats
  Without repugnancy? If there be   45
  Such valor in the bearing, what make we
  Abroad? Why then, women are more valiant
  That stay at home, if bearing carry it;   48
  And the ass more captain than the lion; the fellow
  Loaden with irons wiser than the judge,   50
  If wisdom be in suffering. O my lords,
  As you are great, be pitifully good.
  Who cannot condemn rashness in cold blood?
  To kill, I grant, is sin's extremest gust;   54
  But in defense, by mercy, 'tis most just.   55
  To be in anger is impiety;
  But who is man that is not angry?   57
  Weigh but the crime with this.
SECOND SENATOR
  You breathe in vain.
ALCIBIADES   In vain? His service done
  At Lacedaemon and Byzantium   60
  Were a sufficient briber for his life.
FIRST SENATOR
  What's that?

---

38 *clear* innocent   39 *bear* put up with wrongs is valor   42 *fond* foolish   43
sleep why do they not sleep   45 *repugnancy* resistance   48 *bearing* enduring
(with pun on the meaning "childbearing")   54 *gust* (1) outburst, (2) ap-
petite   55 *by mercy* if we but take a merciful view of it   57 *not* never

ALCIBIADES
    Why, I say, my lords, he's done fair service
    And slain in fight many of your enemies.
    How full of valor did he bear himself
    In the last conflict, and made plenteous wounds!
SECOND SENATOR
    He has made too much plenty with 'em.
68   He's a sworn rioter; he has a sin that often
    Drowns him and takes his valor prisoner.
70   If there were no foes, that were enough
    To overcome him. In that beastly fury
    He has been known to commit outrages
73   And cherish factions. 'Tis inferred to us
    His days are foul and his drink dangerous.
FIRST SENATOR
    He dies.
ALCIBIADES   Hard fate! He might have died in war.
76   My lords, if not for any parts in him –
77   Though his right arm might purchase his own time,
    And be in debt to none – yet, more to move you,
    Take my deserts to his and join 'em both;
80   And, for I know your reverend ages love
81   Security, I'll pawn my victories, all
    My honor to you, upon his good returns.
    If by this crime he owes the law his life,
84   Why, let the war receive't in valiant gore;
    For law is strict, and war is nothing more.
FIRST SENATOR
    We are for law. He dies. Urge it no more,
87   On height of our displeasure. Friend or brother,
88   He forfeits his own blood that spills another.

---

68 *sworn rioter* confirmed disorderly drunk   70 *that* i.e., the sin of drunkenness   73 *cherish factions* foster dissension; *inferred* alleged   76 *parts* good qualities   77 *his own time* the right to a natural death when his time comes   81 *Security* (1) safety, (2) collateral (hence *pawn* and *good returns*)   84 *let . . . gore* i.e., let him give it in battle   87 *On height of our* on pain of our highest   88 *another* i.e., another's blood

ALCIBIADES
    Must it be so? It must not be. My lords,
    I do beseech you know me.   90
SECOND SENATOR   How?
ALCIBIADES
    Call me to your remembrances.
THIRD SENATOR   What!
ALCIBIADES
    I cannot think but your age has forgot me;
    It could not else be I should prove so base,
    To sue and be denied such common grace.   94
    My wounds ache at you.
FIRST SENATOR   Do you dare our anger?
    'Tis in few words but spacious in effect:
    We banish thee for ever.
ALCIBIADES   Banish me?
    Banish your dotage, banish usury,
    That makes the Senate ugly!
FIRST SENATOR
    If after two days' shine Athens contain thee,   100
    Attend our weightier judgment. And, not to swell our   101
       spirit,
    He shall be executed presently.   *Exeunt [Senators].*   102
ALCIBIADES
    Now the gods keep you old enough that you may live   103
    Only in bone, that none may look on you!
    I'm worse than mad: I have kept back their foes
    While they have told their money and let out   106
    Their coin upon large interest, I myself
    Rich only in large hurts. All those for this?
    Is this the balsam that the usuring Senate
    Pours into captains' wounds? Banishment!   110
    It comes not ill; I hate not to be banished;

---

94 *To . . . denied* that I should ask for and be refused 101 *Attend . . . judgment* expect our more severe sentence; *spirit* anger 102 *presently* immediately 103–4 *live . . . bone* be mere skeletons 106 *told* counted

It is a cause worthy my spleen and fury,
That I may strike at Athens. I'll cheer up
114   My discontented troops and lay for hearts.
'Tis honor with most lands to be at odds;
116   Soldiers should brook as little wrongs as gods.   *Exit.*

                                   *

∾ **III.6** *[Music. Tables set out, Servants attending.]*
Enter divers Friends [of Timon, being Senators and
Lords,] at several doors.

FIRST FRIEND   The good time of day to you, sir.

SECOND FRIEND   I also wish it to you. I think this honorable lord did but try us this other day.

4   FIRST FRIEND   Upon that were my thoughts tiring when we encountered. I hope it is not so low with him as he made it seem in the trial of his several friends.

7   SECOND FRIEND   It should not be, by the persuasion of his new feasting.

FIRST FRIEND   I should think so. He hath sent me an
10   earnest inviting, which many my near occasions did
11   urge me to put off; but he hath conjured me beyond them, and I must needs appear.

13   SECOND FRIEND   In like manner was I in debt to my importunate business, but he would not hear my excuse. I am sorry, when he sent to borrow of me, that my provision was out.

FIRST FRIEND   I am sick of that grief too, as I understand how all things go.

SECOND FRIEND   Every man here's so. What would he
20   have borrowed of you?

FIRST FRIEND   A thousand pieces.

---

114 *lay for hearts* try to win their loyalty   116 *as gods* as do gods
    III.6 The hall of Timon's house   4 *tiring* feeding (a term in falconry)
7 *persuasion* evidence   10 *my near occasions* pressing interests of mine   11
put off decline   11–12 *conjured . . . them* enticed me away from them   13–
14 *was . . . business* did my own affairs make urgent demands of me

SECOND FRIEND   A thousand pieces!

FIRST FRIEND   What of you?

SECOND FRIEND   He sent to me, sir – Here he comes.
　　Enter Timon and Attendants.

TIMON   With all my heart, gentlemen both! And how   25
　　fare you?

FIRST FRIEND   Ever at the best, hearing well of your lord-
　　ship.

SECOND FRIEND   The swallow follows not summer more
　　willing than we your lordship.   30

TIMON   *[Aside]* Nor more willingly leaves winter; such
　　summer birds are men. – Gentlemen, our dinner will
　　not recompense this long stay. Feast your ears with the
　　music awhile, if they will fare so harshly o' th' trumpets'   34
　　sound; we shall to't presently.

FIRST FRIEND   I hope it remains not unkindly with your   36
　　lordship that I returned you an empty messenger.

TIMON   O sir, let it not trouble you.

SECOND FRIEND   My noble lord –

TIMON   Ah, my good friend, what cheer?   40

SECOND FRIEND   My most honorable lord, I am e'en sick
　　of shame that when your lordship this other day sent to
　　me I was so unfortunate a beggar.   43

TIMON   Think not on't, sir.

SECOND FRIEND   If you had sent but two hours before –

TIMON   Let it not cumber your better remembrance.   46
　　(Servants bring in the banquet, then leave.) Come, bring
　　in all together.

SECOND FRIEND   All covered dishes!   49

FIRST FRIEND   Royal cheer, I warrant you.   50

THIRD FRIEND   Doubt not that, if money and the season
　　can yield it.

---

25 *With . . . heart* my cordial greetings   34 *so harshly o'* on such rough fare as
36–37 *it remains . . . messenger* you don't harbor unkind thoughts toward me
because I sent your man back without any money   43 *so . . . beggar* so un-
lucky as to be out of funds   46 *cumber . . . remembrance* trouble you   49
covered (implying especially good food)

FIRST FRIEND   How do you? What's the news?

THIRD FRIEND   Alcibiades is banished. Hear you of it?

BOTH   Alcibiades banished?

THIRD FRIEND   'Tis so, be sure of it.

FIRST FRIEND   How? how?

58 SECOND FRIEND   I pray you, upon what?

TIMON   My worthy friends, will you draw near?

60 THIRD FRIEND   I'll tell you more anon. Here's a noble
61   feast toward.

SECOND FRIEND   This is the old man still.

63 THIRD FRIEND   Will't hold? Will't hold?

SECOND FRIEND   It does; but time will – and so –

65 THIRD FRIEND   I do conceive.

TIMON   Each man to his stool, with that spur as he
67   would to the lip of his mistress. Your diet shall be in all
places alike; make not a city feast of it, to let the meat
cool ere we can agree upon the first place; sit, sit. The
70   gods require our thanks.

You great benefactors, sprinkle our society with thank-
fulness. For your own gifts make yourselves praised;
73   but reserve still to give, lest your deities be despised.
Lend to each man enough, that one need not lend to
another; for were your godheads to borrow of men,
men would forsake the gods. Make the meat be
beloved more than the man that gives it. Let no assem-
bly of twenty be without a score of villains. If there sit
twelve women at the table, let a dozen of them be – as
80   they are. The rest of your fees, O gods – the senators of
81   Athens, together with the common lag of people –
what is amiss in them, you gods, make suitable for de-
83   struction. For these my present friends, as they are to

---

58 *upon what* why   61 *toward* in prospect   63 *hold* last   65 *conceive* get
your idea   67–68 *Your . . . places* i.e., let's be informal and not waste time ar-
guing about who is entitled by rank to sit where, as at an official city dinner
73 *reserve still* always keep something more   80 *fees* property, livestock   81
lag dregs   83 *For* as for

me nothing, so in nothing bless them, and to nothing
are they welcome.

Uncover, dogs, and lap.
    [The dishes are uncovered, and seen to be full of warm
    water and stones.]
SOME SPEAK
  What does his lordship mean?
SOME OTHER   I know not.
TIMON
  May you a better feast never behold,
  You knot of mouth-friends! Smoke and lukewarm water   89
  Is your perfection. This is Timon's last;   90
  Who, stuck and spangled with your flatteries,   91
  Washes it off and sprinkles in your faces
    [Throws the water in their faces.]
  Your reeking villainy. Live loathed and long,
  Most smiling, smooth, detested parasites,
  Courteous destroyers, affable wolves, meek bears,
  You fools of fortune, trencher-friends, time's flies,   96
  Cap-and-knee slaves, vapors, and minute jacks!   97
  Of man and beast the infinite malady   98
  Crust you quite o'er! What, dost thou go?
  Soft, take thy physic first; thou too, and thou!   100
  Stay, I will lend thee money, borrow none.
    [Throws stones and drives them out.]
  What, all in motion? Henceforth be no feast
  Whereat a villain's not a welcome guest.
  Burn house! Sink Athens! Henceforth hated be
  Of Timon man and all humanity!   *Exit.*
    Enter the Senators with other Lords.

---

89 *mouth-friends* flatterers and parasites; *Smoke* steam ("hot air") 90 *Is your perfection* suits you best 91 *spangled* decorated, sparkling 96 *time's flies* fair-weather insects 97 *Cap-and-knee* insincerely deferential (see IV.3.211–14); *vapors* creatures without substance; *minute jacks* timeservers 98–99 *the infinite . . . o'er* every possible disease cover you wholly with scabs 100 *physic* medicine

FIRST FRIEND   How now, my lords?

SECOND FRIEND   Know you the quality of Lord Timon's
fury?

109   THIRD FRIEND   Push! Did you see my cap?

110   FOURTH FRIEND   I have lost my gown.

111   FIRST FRIEND   He's but a mad lord and nought but humors sways him. He gave me a jewel th' other day, and
now he has beat it out of my hat. Did you see my jewel?

THIRD FRIEND   Did you see my cap?

SECOND FRIEND   Here 'tis.

FOURTH FRIEND   Here lies my gown.

FIRST FRIEND   Let's make no stay.

SECOND FRIEND
Lord Timon's mad.

THIRD FRIEND   I feel't upon my bones.

FOURTH FRIEND
One day he gives us diamonds, next day stones.

Exeunt.

*

~ IV.1 *Enter Timon.*

TIMON
Let me look back upon thee. O thou wall
That girdles in those wolves, dive in the earth
3   And fence not Athens! Matrons, turn incontinent!
Obedience fail in children! Slaves and fools,
Pluck the grave wrinkled Senate from the bench
6   And minister in their steads! To general filths
Convert o' th' instant, green virginity!
Do't in your parents' eyes! Bankrupts, hold fast;

---

109 *Push* humph! (an expression of irritation or contempt)   111–12 *humors*
whims (see I.2.26 n.)
   IV.1 Outside the walls of Athens   3 *incontinent* promiscuous   6 *general
filths* common whores

Rather than render back, out with your knives
And cut your trusters' throats! Bound servants, steal: 10
Large-handed robbers your grave masters are   11
And pill by law. Maid, to thy master's bed: 12
Thy mistress is o' th' brothel. Son of sixteen,
Pluck the lined crutch from thy old limping sire;   14
With it beat out his brains! Piety and fear,
Religion to the gods, peace, justice, truth,   16
Domestic awe, night-rest and neighborhood,   17
Instruction, manners, mysteries and trades,   18
Degrees, observances, customs and laws,   19
Decline to your confounding contraries,   20
And yet confusion live! Plagues incident to men,
Your potent and infectious fevers heap
On Athens, ripe for stroke! Thou cold sciatica,   23
Cripple our senators, that their limbs may halt   24
As lamely as their manners! Lust and liberty   25
Creep in the minds and marrows of our youth,
That 'gainst the stream of virtue they may strive
And drown themselves in riot! Itches, blains,   28
Sow all th' Athenian bosoms, and their crop
Be general leprosy! Breath infect breath,   30
That their society, as their friendship, may
Be merely poison! Nothing I'll bear from thee   32
But nakedness, thou detestable town;
Take thou that too, with multiplying bans!   34
Timon will to the woods, where he shall find
Th' unkindest beast more kinder than mankind.

---

10 *Bound* indentured, under a contract to serve for a set number of years
11 *Large-handed* i.e., sticky-fingered 12 *pill* rob 14 *lined* padded 16 *Re-ligion to* veneration of 17 *Domestic awe* respect for parents; *neighborhood* neighborliness 18 *mysteries* crafts 19 *Degrees* ranks 20–21 *Decline . . . live* degenerate into chaos, and may confusion then persist 23 *sciatica* pain in the sciatic nerve, which runs down the leg, often associated with age 24 *halt* limp 25 *liberty* license 28 *blains* blisters, boils (many of the afflictions Timon wishes on the Athenians are associated with sexually transmitted disease) 32 *merely* pure 34 *that too* (another article of clothing); *bans* curses

The gods confound – hear me, you good gods all –
Th' Athenians both within and out that wall;
And grant, as Timon grows, his hate may grow
40   To the whole race of mankind, high and low!
Amen.   *Exit.*

*

∽ **IV.2** *Enter [Flavius the] Steward with two or three*
Servants.

FIRST SERVANT
   Hear you, Master Steward, where's our master?
   Are we undone? cast off? nothing remaining?
STEWARD
   Alack, my fellows, what should I say to you?
   Let me be recorded by the righteous gods,
   I am as poor as you.
FIRST SERVANT   Such a house broke?
   So noble a master fall'n; all gone, and not
7   One friend to take his fortune by the arm
   And go along with him?
SECOND SERVANT   As we do turn our backs
9   From our companion thrown into his grave,
10.   So his familiars to his buried fortunes
   Slink all away; leave their false vows with him,
   Like empty purses picked; and his poor self,
13   A dedicated beggar to the air,
   With his disease of all-shunned poverty,
15   Walks, like contempt, alone. More of our fellows.
      Enter other Servants.
STEWARD
   All broken implements of a ruined house.

IV.2 The house of Timon   7 *his fortune* i.e., him, in his misfortune
9 *From . . . grave* from the grave of a newly buried friend   13 *dedicated . . .*
air beggar who has pledged himself to the open air   15 *like contempt* as if he
were contempt itself

THIRD SERVANT
   Yet do our hearts wear Timon's livery;
   That see I by our faces. We are fellows still,
   Serving alike in sorrow. Leaked is our bark;
   And we, poor mates, stand on the dying deck,   20
   Hearing the surges threat. We must all part   21
   Into this sea of air.

STEWARD   Good fellows all,
   The latest of my wealth I'll share amongst you.   23
   Wherever we shall meet, for Timon's sake
   Let's yet be fellows; let's shake our heads and say,
   As 'twere a knell unto our master's fortunes,
   "We have seen better days." Let each take some.
     [Gives money.]
   Nay, put out all your hands. Not one word more;   28
   Thus part we rich in sorrow, parting poor.
     Embrace, and part several ways.

   O the fierce wretchedness that glory brings us!   30
   Who would not wish to be from wealth exempt,
   Since riches point to misery and contempt?
   Who would be so mocked with glory, or to live
   But in a dream of friendship,
   To have his pomp and all what state compounds   35
   But only painted, like his varnished friends?   36
   Poor honest lord, brought low by his own heart,
   Undone by goodness! Strange, unusual blood,   38
   When man's worst sin is he does too much good!
   Who then dares to be half so kind again?   40
   For bounty, that makes gods, does still mar men.
   My dearest lord, blessed to be most accursed,   42
   Rich only to be wretched, thy great fortunes
   Are made thy chief afflictions. Alas, kind lord,

---

19 *bark* small boat **20** *dying* i.e., sinking **21** *surges* waves **21–22** *part . . . air* depart into this expanse of nothingness, death **23** *The latest* what remains **28** *put out all* all of you put out **35** *what state compounds* that splendor consists of **36** *But only* nothing more than **38** *blood* nature **40** *again* hereafter **42** *to be* only to be

45   He's flung in rage from this ingrateful seat
46   Of monstrous friends; nor has he with him to
47   Supply his life, or that which can command it.
      I'll follow and inquire him out.
      I'll ever serve his mind with my best will;
50   Whilst I have gold, I'll be his steward still.   *Exit.*

                                        *

∾ **IV.3** *Enter Timon in the woods.*

TIMON
      O blessèd breeding sun, draw from the earth
2   Rotten humidity; below thy sister's orb
      Infect the air! Twinned brothers of one womb –
      Whose procreation, residence, and birth
5   Scarce is dividant – touch them with several fortunes,
6   The greater scorns the lesser. Not nature,
      To whom all sores lay siege, can bear great fortune
8   But by contempt of nature.
9   Raise me this beggar and deny't that lord;
10   The senator shall bear contempt hereditary,
      The beggar native honor.
12   It is the pasture lards the brother's sides,
      The want that makes him lean. Who dares, who dares
      In purity of manhood stand upright
      And say "This man's a flatterer"? If one be,
16   So are they all; for every grise of fortune

---

45 *seat* site, home   46–47 *to / Supply* what is needed to sustain   47 *that . . .
it* i.e., money
    IV.3 Before Timon's cave in a wood by the sea   2 *thy sister's* the moon's
5 *dividant* divisible   6 *The* so that the   6–7 *Not nature . . . can* human nature . . . cannot   8 *nature* natural ties   9 *deny't* withhold such elevation
from   10–11 *The senator . . . honor* i.e., let each be treated as if born to what
he now merits   12–13 *It . . . lean* (probably a comparison of the fortunes of
firstborn and younger brothers under primogeniture, which confers family
property on the eldest son; inheriting land *lards*, or fattens, one brother, even
as his younger brother starves for want of inheritance)   16–17 *every . . .
below* each rank or step (*grise*) is flattered by the next lower one

Is smoothed by that below. The learnèd pate
Ducks to the golden fool. All's obliquy;   18
There's nothing level in our cursèd natures   19
But direct villainy. Therefore be abhorred   20
All feasts, societies, and throngs of men.
His semblable, yea himself, Timon disdains.   22
Destruction fang mankind! Earth, yield me roots;   23
      [Digs.]
Who seeks for better of thee, sauce his palate
With thy most operant poison. What is here?   25
Gold? Yellow, glittering, precious gold!
No, gods, I am no idle votarist: 27
Roots, you clear heavens! Thus much of this will make   28
Black white, foul fair, wrong right,
Base noble, old young, coward valiant.   30
Ha, you gods, why this? What this, you gods? Why, this
Will lug your priests and servants from your sides,
Pluck stout men's pillows from below their heads.
This yellow slave
Will knit and break religions, bless th' accursed,
Make the hoar leprosy adored, place thieves   36
And give them title, knee, and approbation   37
With senators on the bench. This is it
That makes the wappened widow wed again;   39
She whom the spital house and ulcerous sores   40
Would cast the gorge at, this embalms and spices   41
To th' April day again. Come, damned earth,   42
Thou common whore of mankind, that puts odds   43

---

18 *golden* rich; *obliquy* indirectness **19** *level* straightforward **22** *His sem-blable* anything like him **23** *fang* seize **25** *operant* potent **27** *idle votarist* insincere worshiper (I meant it when I asked for roots) **28** *clear* pure **36** *hoar* white (as lepers' skins are, with a pun on "whore" to reinforce the link between women and disease); *place* give high office to **37** *knee* deference (shown by kneeling to) **39** *wappened* worn out **40–41** *whom . . . gorge at* at the mere sight of whom hospital patients with running sores would vomit **41** *embalms* preserves, restores **42** *damned earth* i.e., gold **43–44** *puts odds / Among* sets at each other's throats

Among the rout of nations, I will make thee
45 Do thy right nature.
        March afar off.   Ha! a drum? Thou'rt quick;
46 But yet I'll bury thee. Thou'lt go, strong thief,
When gouty keepers of thee cannot stand.
48 Nay, stay thou out for earnest.
        [Keeps some gold.]
        Enter Alcibiades, with Drum and Fife, in warlike
        manner; and Phrynia and Timandra.

ALCIBIADES   What art thou there?
Speak.

TIMON
50 A beast, as thou art. The canker gnaw thy heart
For showing me again the eyes of man!

ALCIBIADES
What is thy name? Is man so hateful to thee
That art thyself a man?

TIMON
I am Misanthropos and hate mankind.
For thy part, I do wish thou wert a dog,
56 That I might love thee something.

ALCIBIADES   I know thee well,
57 But in thy fortunes am unlearned and strange.

TIMON
I know thee too; and more than that I know thee
I not desire to know. Follow thy drum;
60 With man's blood paint the ground, gules, gules!
Religious canons, civil laws are cruel;
62 Then what should war be? This fell whore of thine
Hath in her more destruction than thy sword
64 For all her cherubin look.

---

45 *thy right nature* your proper work (of corrupting mankind); *quick* (1)
swift, (2) alive (hence unburied) 46 *go* walk 48 *for earnest* as "earnest
money," a down payment or collateral (cf. IV.3.168) 48 s.d. *Drum and Fife*
drummer and fifer 50 *canker* cancerous disease 56 *something* a little 57
unlearned and strange uninformed and ignorant (but cf. ll.77, 93–96) 60
gules red (in heraldry) 62 *fell* deadly 64 *cherubin* angelic

PHRYNIA   Thy lips rot off!

TIMON

  I will not kiss thee; then the rot returns

  To thine own lips again.

ALCIBIADES

  How came the noble Timon to this change?

TIMON

  As the moon does, by wanting light to give.   68

  But then renew I could not, like the moon;

  There were no suns to borrow of.   70

ALCIBIADES   Noble Timon,

  What friendship may I do thee?

TIMON   None, but to

  Maintain my opinion.   72

ALCIBIADES   What is it, Timon?

TIMON Promise me friendship, but perform none. If   73
thou wilt not promise, the gods plague thee, for thou
art a man! if thou dost perform, confound thee, for
thou art a man!

ALCIBIADES

  I have heard in some sort of thy miseries.   77

TIMON

  Thou saw'st them when I had prosperity.

ALCIBIADES

  I see them now; then was a blessèd time.

TIMON

  As thine is now, held with a brace of harlots.   80

TIMANDRA

  Is this th' Athenian minion whom the world   81

  Voiced so regardfully?   82

TIMON   Art thou Timandra?

TIMANDRA Yes.

---

68 *wanting* lacking **72** *Maintain* confirm (of mankind) **73–76** *If . . . man*
if you are a man you deserve damnation even if you do not make false
promises, and even if you do what you promise to **77** *in some sort* a little
(but see ll. 57 and 93–96) **81** *minion* darling **82** *Voiced* spoke of

TIMON
      Be a whore still. They love thee not that use thee;
85   Give them diseases, leaving with thee their lust.
86   Make use of thy salt hours. Season the slaves
87   For tubs and baths; bring down rose-cheeked youth
      To the tub fast and the diet.
TIMANDRA   Hang thee, monster!
ALCIBIADES
      Pardon him, sweet Timandra; for his wits
90   Are drowned and lost in his calamities.
      I have but little gold of late, brave Timon,
      The want whereof doth daily make revolt
93   In my penurious band. I have heard, and grieved,
      How cursèd Athens, mindless of thy worth,
      Forgetting thy great deeds when neighbor states,
      But for thy sword and fortune, trod upon them –
TIMON
      I prithee beat thy drum and get thee gone.
ALCIBIADES
      I am thy friend and pity thee, dear Timon.
TIMON
      How dost thou pity him whom thou dost trouble?
100   I had rather be alone.
ALCIBIADES   Why, fare thee well.
      Here is some gold for thee.
TIMON   Keep it; I cannot eat it.
ALCIBIADES
102   When I have laid proud Athens on a heap –
TIMON
      Warr'st thou 'gainst Athens?
ALCIBIADES   Ay, Timon, and have cause.

---

85 *leaving . . . lust* (just as they leave their lust behind with you) 86 *salt*
lustful 87 *tubs and baths* (used to treat sexually transmitted diseases by pro-
moting sweating; cf. in l. 88 *tub fast,* abstinence from sex and/or rich foods
during the treatment) 93 *penurious* poverty-stricken 102 *on a heap* in
ruins

TIMON
    The gods confound them all in thy conquest,
    And thee after, when thou hast conquerèd!
ALCIBIADES
    Why me, Timon?
TIMON   That by killing of villains
    Thou wast born to conquer my country.
    Put up thy gold. Go on. Here's gold. Go on.
    Be as a planetary plague when Jove   109
    Will o'er some high-viced city hang his poison   110
    In the sick air. Let not thy sword skip one.
    Pity not honored age for his white beard;
    He is an usurer. Strike me the counterfeit matron;   113
    It is her habit only that is honest,   114
    Herself's a bawd. Let not the virgin's cheek
    Make soft thy trenchant sword; for those milk paps   116
    That through the window bars bore at men's eyes   117
    Are not within the leaf of pity writ,   118
    But set them down horrible traitors. Spare not the babe
    Whose dimpled smiles from fools exhaust their mercy;   120
    Think it a bastard whom the oracle
    Hath doubtfully pronounced the throat shall cut,   122
    And mince it sans remorse. Swear against objects;   123
    Put armor on thine ears and on thine eyes,
    Whose proof nor yells of mothers, maids, nor babes,   125
    Nor sight of priests in holy vestments bleeding,
    Shall pierce a jot. There's gold to pay thy soldiers;

---

109 *planetary* (the plagues London suffered were often attributed to the baleful influence of planets "in opposition") **113** *counterfeit matron* woman pretending married respectability **114** *habit* garb; *honest* chaste **116** *trenchant* sharp; *milk paps* breasts (with reference to nursing, which cuts against "virgin" in the preceding line, and with an emphasis on milky whiteness) **117** *window bars* latticework of the bodice (?) **118** *Are . . . writ* have nothing to do with pity **122** *doubtfully* ambiguously; *the . . . cut* shall grow up to cut throats **123** *mince* chop it to bits; *sans remorse* without pity; *objects* things that evoke pity **125** *proof* tested strength (the armor's)

128   Make large confusion; and, thy fury spent,
Confounded be thyself! Speak not; be gone.

ALCIBIADES

130   Hast thou gold yet? I'll take the gold thou givest me,
Not all thy counsel.

TIMON

Dost thou, or dost thou not, heaven's curse upon thee!

BOTH [WOMEN]

Give us some gold, good Timon. Hast thou more?

TIMON

Enough to make a whore forswear her trade,
135   And, to make whores, a bawd. Hold up, you sluts,
136   Your aprons mountant. You are not oathable,
137   Although I know you'll swear, terribly swear,
138   Into strong shudders and to heavenly agues,
      Th' immortal gods that hear you. Spare your oaths;
140   I'll trust to your conditions. Be whores still;
      And he whose pious breath seeks to convert you –
142   Be strong in whore, allure him, burn him up,
143   Let your close fire predominate his smoke,
144   And be no turncoats. Yet may your pains six months
145   Be quite contrary! And thatch your poor thin roofs
      With burdens of the dead – some that were hanged,
      No matter; wear them, betray with them. Whore still;

---

128 *large confusion* wholesale ruin 135 *to . . . bawd* to make a bawd stop making women into whores 136 *mountant* ever-rising (a new word coined in imitation of heraldic terms such as "rampant" and "couchant"); *oathable* believable 137 *swear* (to do what I shall ask) 138 *strong . . . agues* symptoms of both orgasm and sexually transmitted disease 140 *your conditions* what you are 142 *burn* enflame with desire, infect, make sting as a result of infection 143 *Let . . . smoke* let the hidden flames of desire overcome his pious "hot air" (cf. III.6.89); infect or conquer him 144–45 *Yet . . . contrary* (confusing; while Timon applauds the misery prostitutes spread, he wants them to suffer, too) 145–46 *thatch . . . dead* cover your baldness with hair taken from corpses

Paint till a horse may mire upon your face.   148
A pox of wrinkles!
BOTH   Well, more gold! What then?
Believe't that we'll do anything for gold.   150
TIMON
Consumptions sow
In hollow bones of man; strike their sharp shins,
And mar men's spurring. Crack the lawyer's voice,   153
That he may never more false title plead
Nor sound his quillets shrilly. Hoar the flamen,   155
That scolds against the quality of flesh   156
And not believes himself. Down with the nose –   157
Down with it flat; take the bridge quite away –
Of him that, his particular to foresee,   159
Smells from the general weal. Make curled-pate ruffi-   160
ans bald,
And let the unscarred braggarts of the war
Derive some pain from you. Plague all,
That your activity may defeat and quell   163
The source of all erection. There's more gold.   164
Do you damn others and let this damn you,
And ditches grave you all!   166
BOTH
More counsel with more money, bounteous Timon.

---

148 *mire upon* bog down in (Timon advises the women to cover up the consequences of disease with wigs [ll. 145–46] and makeup, so that they may
lure and infect even more men) **153** *mar . . . spurring* make them less capa-
ble of vigorous riding or lovemaking **155** *quillets* quibbles; *Hoar the flamen*
whiten (with leprosy) the priest **156** *the . . . flesh* fleshly desire **157–59**
Down . . . Of i.e., let syphilis afflict **159–60** *his . . . weal* in hunting after
private gain loses scent of the common good **163** *quell* destroy **164** *erection* professional or social advancement, or sexual arousal (let disease lead to
ruin and impotence) (in this scene, Timon repeatedly refers to the symptoms
of advanced syphilis and the side effects of treating it with mercury: baldness,
an eroded nose, impotence, general debility) **166** *grave* entomb

TIMON

168　More whore, more mischief first; I have given you
　　earnest.

ALCIBIADES

　　Strike up the drum towards Athens! Farewell, Timon;

170　If I thrive well, I'll visit thee again.

TIMON

171　If I hope well, I'll never see thee more.

ALCIBIADES

　　I never did thee harm.

TIMON

　　Yes, thou spok'st well of me.

ALCIBIADES　　　　　　　　　　　Call'st thou that harm?

TIMON

174　Men daily find it. Get thee away and take
　　Thy beagles with thee.

ALCIBIADES　　　　　　　We but offend him. Strike!
　　　　　　　　　[Drum beats.] Exeunt [all but Timon].

TIMON

　　That nature, being sick of man's unkindness,
　　Should yet be hungry! Common mother, thou
　　　[Digs.]
　　Whose womb unmeasurable and infinite breast

179　Teems and feeds all; whose selfsame mettle

180　Whereof thy proud child, arrogant man, is puffed
　　Engenders the black toad and adder blue,
　　The gilded newt and eyeless venomed worm,

183　With all th' abhorrèd births below crisp heaven

184　Whereon Hyperion's quick'ning fire doth shine –
　　Yield him who all the human sons do hate,
　　From forth thy plenteous bosom, one poor root!

187　Ensear thy fertile and conceptious womb;

---

168 *earnest* a token payment **171** *If . . . well* if my hopes are realized **174**
find it learn that it is **179** *Teems* prolifically brings forth; *mettle* essence
183 *crisp* clear **184** *Hyperion's quick'ning* the sun's life-giving **187** *Ensear*
dry up

Let it no more bring out ingrateful man!
Go great with tigers, dragons, wolves, and bears;   189
Teem with new monsters whom thy upward face   190
Hath to the marbled mansion all above
Never presented! – O, a root! Dear thanks! –
Dry up thy marrows, vines, and plow-torn leas,   193
Whereof ingrateful man with liquorish draughts   194
And morsels unctuous greases his pure mind,   195
That from it all consideration slips –   196
   Enter Apemantus.
More man? Plague, plague!

APEMANTUS
I was directed hither. Men report
Thou dost affect my manners and dost use them.   199

TIMON
'Tis then because thou dost not keep a dog,   *200*
Whom I would imitate. Consumption catch thee!

APEMANTUS
This is in thee a nature but infected,
A poor unmanly melancholy sprung
From change of future. Why this spade? this place?
This slavelike habit and these looks of care?   205
Thy flatterers yet wear silk, drink wine, lie soft,
Hug their diseased perfumes, and have forgot   207
That ever Timon was. Shame not these woods
By putting on the cunning of a carper.   209
Be thou a flatterer now and seek to thrive   *210*
By that which has undone thee; hinge thy knee
And let his very breath whom thou'lt observe   212
Blow off thy cap; praise his most vicious strain

---

189 *Go great* be pregnant   190–92 *whom . . . presented* i.e., hitherto un-
known   193 *leas* fields   194 *liquorish* tempting, lecherous   195 *greases* (1)
oils, (2) makes lewd   196 *consideration* ability to think   199 *affect* assume
205 *habit* garb (cf. IV.1.32–34), but also way of life (cf. IV.3.239)   207 *diseased perfumes* perfumed but diseased mistresses   209 *putting on . . . carper*
pretending to a cynic's art – i.e., Apemantus's own role (cf. l.218)   212 *observe* court

And call it excellent. Thou wast told thus;
Thou gav'st thine ears, like tapsters that bade welcome,
To knaves and all approachers. 'Tis most just
That thou turn rascal; hadst thou wealth again,
Rascals should have't. Do not assume my likeness.

TIMON
Were I like thee, I'd throw away myself.

APEMANTUS
220   Thou hast cast away thyself, being like thyself;
A madman so long, now a fool. What, think'st
222   That the bleak air, thy boisterous chamberlain,
Will put thy shirt on warm? Will these moist trees,
224   That have outlived the eagle, page thy heels
And skip when thou point'st out? Will the cold brook,
226   Candied with ice, caudle thy morning taste
227   To cure thy o'ernight's surfeit? Call the creatures
228   Whose naked natures live in all the spite
229   Of wreakful heaven, whose bare unhousèd trunks,
230   To the conflicting elements exposed,
231   Answer mere nature; bid them flatter thee.
232   O, thou shalt find –   A fool of thee. Depart.

TIMON

APEMANTUS
I love thee better now than e'er I did.

TIMON
I hate thee worse.

APEMANTUS   Why?

TIMON   Thou flatter'st misery.

APEMANTUS
235   I flatter not, but say thou art a caitiff.

222–23 *chamberlain . . . warm* valet will warm your shirt before you put it
on   224 *eagle* (proverbially long-lived)   224–25 *page . . . out* serve you as a
page and jump to do your bidding   226 *Candied* crusted over; *caudle . . .
taste* warm your breakfast drink   227 *o'ernight's surfeit* hangover   228 *live in*
are continually exposed to   229 *wreakful* vengeful   231 *Answer mere nature*
must cope with nature in its crudest form   232 *of* in   235 *caitiff* (1) captive,
(2) person in a sorry state, (3) low-status person

TIMON

    Why dost thou seek me out?

APEMANTUS   To vex thee.

TIMON

    Always a villain's office or a fool's.

    Dost please thyself in't?   238

APEMANTUS   Ay.

TIMON   What, a knave too?

APEMANTUS

    If thou didst put this sour cold habit on   239

    To castigate thy pride, 'twere well; but thou   240

    Dost it enforcedly. Thou'dst courtier be again

    Wert thou not beggar. Willing misery

    Outlives incertain pomp, is crowned before;   243

    The one is filling still, never complete,   244

    The other at high wish; best state, contentless,   245

    Hath a distracted and most wretched being,

    Worse than the worst, content.   247

    Thou shouldst desire to die, being miserable.   248

TIMON

    Not by his breath that is more miserable.   249

    Thou art a slave whom Fortune's tender arm   250

    With favor never clasped, but bred a dog.   251

    Hadst thou, like us from our first swath, proceeded   252

    The sweet degrees that this brief world affords

    To such as may the passive drugs of it   254

    Freely command, thou wouldst have plunged thyself

    In general riot, melted down thy youth

---

238 *knave* a man whose low social status (as servant or subordinate) corresponds to low moral status, and who makes mischief intentionally (as opposed to the fool); *too* i.e., as well as a fool (see l. 237)   239 *put . . . habit on* adopt . . . manner of living   243 *is crowned before* achieves glory sooner   244 *still* always   245 *at high wish* just as desired; *best state, contentless* pomp, which does not bring content   247 *the worst, content* misery, if it is accepted contentedly   248 *miserable* discontented   249 *Not . . . miserable* i.e., not when you are the one recommending this desire   251 *bred a dog* have been a dog from birth   252 *swath* swaddling clothes   254 *drugs* drudges, servants

In different beds of lust, and never learned
The icy precepts of respect, but followed
The sugared game before thee. But myself,
260   Who had the world as my confectionary,
The mouths, the tongues, the eyes, and hearts of men
262   At duty, more than I could frame employment;
That numberless upon me stuck, as leaves
264   Do on the oak, have, with one winter's brush,
265   Fell from their boughs and left me open, bare
266   For every storm that blows – I to bear this,
That never knew but better, is some burden.
268   Thy nature did commence in sufferance; time
Hath made thee hard in't. Why shouldst thou hate men?
270   They never flattered thee. What hast thou given?
If thou wilt curse, thy father, that poor rag,
272   Must be thy subject, who in spite put stuff
To some she-beggar and compounded thee
Poor rogue hereditary. Hence; be gone!
If thou hadst not been born the worst of men,
Thou hadst been a knave and flatterer.

APEMANTUS   Art thou proud yet?

TIMON
Ay, that I am not thee.

APEMANTUS   I, that I was
No prodigal.

TIMON   I, that I am one now.
Were all the wealth I have shut up in thee,
280   I'd give thee leave to hang it. Get thee gone.
That the whole life of Athens were in this!
282   Thus would I eat it.
      [Gnaws a root.]

---

262 *At duty* serving me; *frame* provide with   264 *have* and that have; *win-ter's brush* onslaught of winter   265 *Fell* fallen   266 *I* for me   268 *sufferance* suffering, endurance   272–73 *put stuff / To* had sex with, impregnated   280 *it* i.e., yourself

APEMANTUS   Here! I will mend thy feast.
    [Offers him food.]
TIMON
    First mend my company; take away thyself.
APEMANTUS
    So I shall mend mine own, by th' lack of thine.
TIMON
    'Tis not well mended so; it is but botched.   285
    If not, I would it were.   286
APEMANTUS
    What wouldst thou have to Athens?
TIMON
    Thee thither in a whirlwind. If thou wilt,
    Tell them there I have gold. Look, so I have.
APEMANTUS
    Here is no use for gold.   290
TIMON   The best and truest;
    For here it sleeps, and does no hirèd harm.
APEMANTUS
    Where liest a-nights, Timon?   292
TIMON   Under that's above me.
    Where feed'st thou a-days, Apemantus?
APEMANTUS   Where my stomach finds meat; or rather,
    where I eat it.
TIMON
    Would poison were obedient and knew my mind!
APEMANTUS
    Where wouldst thou send it?
TIMON
    To sauce thy dishes.
APEMANTUS   The middle of humanity thou never knewest,
    but the extremity of both ends. When thou wast in thy   300
    gilt and thy perfume, they mocked thee for too much

---

282 *mend* improve the quality of   285 *botched* badly patched (since you are
still in your own company)   286 *If not* i.e., if not mended to this extent, by
your leaving   292 *that's* what's

302 curiosity; in thy rags thou know'st none, but art despised
303 for the contrary. There's a medlar for thee; eat it.

TIMON   On what I hate I feed not.

APEMANTUS   Dost hate a medlar?

306 TIMON   Ay, though it look like thee.

307 APEMANTUS   An thou'dst hated meddlers sooner, thou
     shouldst have loved thyself better now. What man didst
309 thou ever know unthrift that was beloved after his
310 means?

TIMON   Who, without those means thou talk'st of, didst
     thou ever know beloved?

APEMANTUS   Myself.

TIMON   I understand thee. Thou hadst some means to
     keep a dog.

APEMANTUS   What things in the world canst thou near-
     est compare to thy flatterers?

TIMON   Women nearest; but men – men are the things
     themselves. What wouldst thou do with the world,
320 Apemantus, if it lay in thy power?

APEMANTUS   Give it the beasts, to be rid of the men.

TIMON   Wouldst thou have thyself fall in the confusion
     of men, and remain a beast with the beasts?

APEMANTUS   Ay, Timon.

TIMON   A beastly ambition, which the gods grant thee t'
     attain to! If thou wert the lion, the fox would beguile
     thee; if thou wert the lamb, the fox would eat thee; if
     thou wert the fox, the lion would suspect thee when
     peradventure thou wert accused by the ass; if thou wert
330 the ass, thy dullness would torment thee, and still thou
331 liv'dst but as a breakfast to the wolf. If thou wert the
     wolf thy greediness would afflict thee, and oft thou

---

302 *curiosity* fastidiousness 303 *medlar* small apple, thought to resemble
the vagina or the anus, eaten when rotten (often used, as here, in quibbles on
meddlers in others' affairs) 306 *like thee* i.e., well decayed 307 *An* if; *meddlers* (with a second meaning of those who are sexually very active) 309 *unthrift* (to be a) spendthrift; *after* in accordance with (?), after the loss of (?)
331 *liv'dst* would live

shouldst hazard thy life for thy dinner. Wert thou the
unicorn, pride and wrath would confound thee and   334
make thine own self the conquest of thy fury; wert
thou a bear, thou wouldst be killed by the horse; wert
thou a horse, thou wouldst be seized by the leopard;
wert thou a leopard, thou wert germane to the lion, 338
and the spots of thy kindred were jurors on thy life: all   339
thy safety were remotion and thy defense absence.   340
What beast couldst thou be that were not subject to a
beast? And what a beast art thou already, that seest not
thy loss in transformation!   343

APEMANTUS   If thou couldst please me with speaking to
me, thou might'st have hit upon it here. The common-
wealth of Athens is become a forest of beasts.

TIMON   How has the ass broke the wall, that thou art out
of the city?

APEMANTUS   Yonder comes a poet and a painter. The   349
plague of company light upon thee! I will fear to catch   350
it, and give way. When I know not what else to do, I'll
see thee again.

TIMON   When there is nothing living but thee, thou
shalt be welcome. I had rather be a beggar's dog than
Apemantus.

APEMANTUS

Thou art the cap of all the fools alive.   356

TIMON

Would thou wert clean enough to spit upon!

APEMANTUS

A plague on thee! thou art too bad to curse.

TIMON

All villains that do stand by thee are pure.   359

---

334 *unicorn* (the way to capture this mythical beast was supposedly to pro-
voke it to anger)   338 *germane* akin   339 *spots . . . life* the spots or faults of
your kindred would condemn you to death   340 *remotion* going elsewhere
343 *thy . . . transformation* what you would lose by the change   349 *Yonder . . . painter* (they don't in fact appear until nearly 190 lines later)   356
cap head, chief   359 *by* compared with

APEMANTUS

360   There is no leprosy but what thou speak'st.

TIMON

    If I name thee.

362   I'll beat thee, but I should infect my hands.

APEMANTUS

    I would my tongue could rot them off!

TIMON

    Away, thou issue of a mangy dog!
    Choler does kill me that thou art alive;
    I swoon to see thee.

APEMANTUS   Would thou wouldst burst!

TIMON   Away,
    Thou tedious rogue! I am sorry I shall lose
    A stone by thee.
      [Throws a stone at him.]

APEMANTUS   Beast!

370 TIMON   Slave!

APEMANTUS   Toad!

TIMON

    Rogue, rogue, rogue!
    I am sick of this false world, and will love nought

374   But even the mere necessities upon't.
    Then, Timon, presently prepare thy grave.
    Lie where the light foam of the sea may beat
    Thy gravestone daily. Make thine epitaph,

378   That death in me at others' lives may laugh.
      [To the gold]
    O thou sweet king-killer, and dear divorce

380   'Twixt natural son and sire; thou bright defiler

381   Of Hymen's purest bed; thou valiant Mars;
    Thou ever young, fresh, loved, and delicate wooer,

383   Whose blush doth thaw the consecrated snow

---

362 *I'll* I'd   374 *But even* save only; *necessities* (of which death is the chief: see next line)   378 *death in me* I, though dead   381 *Hymen* the god of marriage; *Mars* the god of war   383 *blush* glow (of the gold, not of Mars)

That lies on Dian's lap; thou visible god,   384
That sold'rest close impossibilities   385
And mak'st them kiss; that speak'st with every tongue
To every purpose! O thou touch of hearts!   387
Think thy slave man rebels; and by thy virtue
Set them into confounding odds, that beasts   389
May have the world in empire!   390

APEMANTUS   Would 'twere so,
But not till I am dead. I'll say thou'st gold.
Thou wilt be thronged to shortly.

TIMON   Thronged to?

APEMANTUS   Ay.

TIMON
Thy back, I prithee.

APEMANTUS   Live, and love thy misery.

TIMON
Long live so, and so die. I am quit.

APEMANTUS
More things like men! Eat, Timon, and abhor them.

                                         Exit Apemantus.

   Enter the Banditti.

FIRST BANDIT Where should he have this gold? It is   396
some poor fragment, some slender ort of his remainder. 397
The mere want of gold and the falling-from of his
friends drove him into this melancholy.

SECOND BANDIT It is noised he hath a mass of treasure.   400

THIRD BANDIT Let us make the assay upon him. If he   401
care not for't, he will supply us easily; if he covetously
reserve it, how shall's get it?   403

SECOND BANDIT True; for he bears it not about him; 'tis
hid.

---

384 *Dian* a virgin goddess, patroness of chastity 385 *sold'rest* welds; *close* firmly together 387 *touch* touchstone (used to test the quality of gold or silver alloys; here gold itself is used to test hearts) 389 *them* all men 396 *should he have* can he have got (?), can he be keeping (?) 397 *ort . . . remainder* scrap of what he had left 401 *make . . . him* try him (in the language of goldsmiths) 403 *shall's* shall we

FIRST BANDIT   Is not this he?
ALL   Where?
SECOND BANDIT   'Tis his description.
THIRD BANDIT   He! I know him.
410   ALL   Save thee, Timon!
TIMON   Now, thieves?
ALL
412   Soldiers, not thieves.
TIMON   Both too, and women's sons.
ALL
      We are not thieves, but men that much do want.
TIMON
414   Your greatest want is, you want much of meat.
      Why should you want? Behold, the earth hath roots;
      Within this mile break forth a hundred springs;
417   The oaks bear mast, the briers scarlet hips;
      The bounteous housewife Nature on each bush
419   Lays her full mess before you. Want? Why want?
FIRST BANDIT
420   We cannot live on grass, on berries, water,
      As beasts and birds and fishes.
TIMON
      Nor on the beasts themselves, the birds and fishes;
423   You must eat men. Yet thanks I must you con
      That you are thieves professed, that you work not
      In holier shapes; for there is boundless theft
426   In limited professions. Rascal thieves,
      Here's gold. Go, suck the subtle blood o' th' grape
428   Till the high fever seethe your blood to froth,
      And so scape hanging. Trust not the physician;
430   His antidotes are poison, and he slays
      More than you rob. Take wealth and lives together.

---

412 *Both too, and* both indeed, and also   414 *Your . . . meat* what you really
need is merely plenty of food   417 *mast* acorns; *hips* fruit of the rose   419
full mess complete menu   423 *thanks* gratitude; *con* acknowledge   426 *limited* regular, legal   428 *high fever seethe* drunkenness boil

Do villainy, do, since you protest to do't,   432
Like workmen. I'll example you with thievery: 433
The sun's a thief, and with his great attraction
Robs the vast sea; the moon's an arrant thief,
And her pale fire she snatches from the sun;
The sea's a thief, whose liquid surge resolves
The moon into salt tears; the earth's a thief,
That feeds and breeds by a composture stol'n   439
From gen'ral excrement. Each thing's a thief.   440
The laws, your curb and whip, in their rough power
Has unchecked theft. Love not yourselves: away,   442
Rob one another. There's more gold. Cut throats.
All that you meet are thieves. To Athens go;
Break open shops; nothing can you steal
But thieves do lose it. Steal less for this I give you,   446
And gold confound you howsoe'er! Amen.   447
THIRD BANDIT   Has almost charmed me from my profes-
sion by persuading me to it.
FIRST BANDIT   'Tis in the malice of mankind that he thus   450
advises us, not to have us thrive in our mystery.   451
SECOND BANDIT   I'll believe him as an enemy, and give   452
over my trade.
FIRST BANDIT   Let us first see peace in Athens; there is no   454
time so miserable but a man may be true.
                              Exit [with the other] Thieves.
     Enter [Flavius] the Steward, to Timon.
STEWARD
   O you gods!
   Is yon despised and ruinous man my lord?
   Full of decay and failing? O monument
   And wonder of good deeds evilly bestowed!

---

432 *protest* profess   433 *example you with* give some examples to justify your
439 *composture* manure   442 *Has . . . theft* have a license to steal   446 *for*
because you have   447 *howsoe'er* anyhow   451 *mystery* craft   452 *as* as I
would   454 *peace* (when thievery is less easy)   454–55 *there . . . true* i.e.,
since one may reform at any time, let's not make any radical changes while
the pickings are so good

460   What an alteration of honor has desp'rate want made!
      What viler thing upon the earth than friends,
      Who can bring noblest minds to basest ends!
463   How rarely does it meet with this time's guise
      When man was wished to love his enemies!
      Grant I may ever love, and rather woo
466   Those that would mischief me than those that do!
      Has caught me in his eye; I will present
      My honest grief unto him, and as my lord
      Still serve him with my life. My dearest master!

TIMON
470   Away! What art thou?

STEWARD   Have you forgot me, sir?

TIMON
      Why dost ask that? I have forgot all men;
      Then if thou grant'st thou'rt a man, I have forgot thee.

STEWARD
      An honest poor servant of yours.

TIMON
      Then I know thee not.
      I never had honest man about me; ay, all
      I kept were knaves, to serve in meat to villains.

STEWARD
      The gods are witness,
      Ne'er did poor steward wear a truer grief
      For his undone lord than mine eyes for you.

TIMON
480   What, dost thou weep? Come nearer then; I love thee
      Because thou art a woman and disclaim'st
482   Flinty mankind, whose eyes do never give
483   But thorough lust and laughter. Pity's sleeping.

463–64 *rarely . . . wished* how appropriate this is at a time when man is urged   466 *Those . . . do* professed enemies than those who harm me though pretending friendship   482 *Flinty* hard; *give* yield tears   483 *But thorough* except through

Strange times, that weep with laughing, not with weep-
    ing!

STEWARD

I beg of you to know me, good my lord,
T' accept my grief, and whilst this poor wealth lasts
To entertain me as your steward still.   487

TIMON

Had I a steward
So true, so just, and now so comfortable?   489
It almost turns my dangerous nature wild.   490
Let me behold thy face. Surely this man
Was born of woman.
Forgive my general and exceptless rashness,   493
You perpetual-sober gods! I do proclaim
One honest man – mistake me not, but one;
No more, I pray – and he's a steward.
How fain would I have hated all mankind,
And thou redeem'st thyself. But all save thee
I fell with curses.
Methinks thou art more honest now than wise;   500
For by oppressing and betraying me
Thou might'st have sooner got another service;
For many so arrive at second masters,
Upon their first lord's neck. But tell me true –
For I must ever doubt, though ne'er so sure –
Is not thy kindness subtle-covetous,
A usuring kindness, and as rich men deal gifts,   507
Expecting in return twenty for one?

STEWARD

No, my most worthy master, in whose breast
Doubt and suspect, alas, are placed too late.   510
You should have feared false times when you did feast.
Suspect still comes where an estate is least.   512

---

487 *entertain* employ   489 *comfortable* comforting   493 *exceptless* making
no exceptions   507 *as* as what we have when   510 *suspect* suspicion   512
still ever

513   That which I show, heaven knows, is merely love,
      Duty, and zeal to your unmatchèd mind,
515   Care of your food and living; and believe it,
      My most honored lord,
517   For any benefit that points to me,
518   Either in hope or present, I'd exchange
      For this one wish, that you had power and wealth
520   To requite me by making rich yourself.

TIMON
521   Look thee, 'tis so! Thou singly honest man,
      Here, take. The gods out of my misery
      Has sent thee treasure. Go, live rich and happy,
524   But thus conditioned: thou shalt build from men,
      Hate all, curse all, show charity to none,
      But let the famished flesh slide from the bone
      Ere thou relieve the beggar. Give to dogs
      What thou deniest to men. Let prisons swallow 'em,
      Debts wither 'em to nothing; be men like blasted woods,
530   And may diseases lick up their false bloods!
      And so farewell, and thrive.

STEWARD   O let me stay
      And comfort you, my master.

TIMON   If thou hat'st curses,
      Stay not; fly, whilst thou art blessed and free;
      Ne'er see thou man, and let me ne'er see thee.
          [Timon withdraws.]   *Exit [Flavius].*

                          *

---

513 *merely* purely   515 *Care of* concern for   517 *points to* may be indicated for   518 *in . . . present* later or now   521 *singly* (1) uniquely, (2) truly   524 *thus conditioned* with these provisos; *from* remote from

❧ **V.1** *Enter Poet and Painter. [Timon watches them from his cave.]*

PAINTER As I took note of the place, it cannot be far where he abides.

POET What's to be thought of him? Does the rumor hold for true that he's so full of gold?

PAINTER Certain. Alcibiades reports it; Phrynia and Timandra had gold of him. He likewise enriched poor straggling soldiers with great quantity. 'Tis said he gave unto his steward a mighty sum.

POET Then this breaking of his has been but a try for his friends? 9 10

PAINTER Nothing else. You shall see him a palm in Athens again, and flourish with the highest. Therefore 'tis not amiss we tender our loves to him in this supposed distress of his; it will show honestly in us and is very likely to load our purposes with what they travail for, if it be a just and true report that goes of his having. 14 15 16

POET What have you now to present unto him?

PAINTER Nothing at this time but my visitation. Only I will promise him an excellent piece.

POET I must serve him so too, tell him of an intent that's coming toward him. 20

PAINTER Good as the best. Promising is the very air o' th' time; it opens the eyes of expectation. Performance is ever the duller for his act; and, but in the plainer and simpler kind of people, the deed of saying is quite out of use. To promise is most courtly and fashionable; performance is a kind of will or testament which argues a great sickness in his judgment that makes it. 24 25

V.1 Before Timon's cave **9** *breaking* going bankrupt; *try* test **14** *show honestly* seem honorable **15** *travail* strive **16** *having* wealth **20–21** *an intent . . . him* what I have in mind for him **24** *for his act* for its being realized; *but* except **25** *deed of saying* fulfillment of promises

Enter Timon from his cave.

TIMON   *[Aside]* Excellent workman! Thou canst not
30   paint a man so bad as is thyself.

POET   I am thinking what I shall say I have provided for
32   him. It must be a personating of himself; a satire
33   against the softness of prosperity, with a discovery of
   the infinite flatteries that follow youth and opulency.

35 TIMON   *[Aside]* Must thou needs stand for a villain in
   thine own work? Wilt thou whip thine own faults in
   other men? Do so, I have gold for thee.

POET   Nay, let's seek him.
   Then do we sin against our own estate
40   When we may profit meet, and come too late.

PAINTER   True.
   When the day serves, before black-cornered night,
   Find what thou want'st by free and offered light.
   Come.

TIMON   *[Aside]*
45   I'll meet you at the turn. What a god's gold
   That he is worshiped in a baser temple
   Than where swine feed!
   'Tis thou that rigg'st the bark and plow'st the foam,
49   Settlest admirèd reverence in a slave.
50   To thee be worship, and thy saints for aye
   Be crowned with plagues, that thee alone obey!
52   Fit I meet them.
     [Comes forward.]

POET
   Hail, worthy Timon!

PAINTER   Our late noble master!

TIMON
54   Have I once lived to see two honest men?

---

32 *a personating of himself* an allegorical representation of his own case **33**
discovery disclosure **35** *stand* serve as a model **45** *meet . . . turn* i.e., give
you a little of your own dishonest game (as he presently does) **49**
Settlest . . . slave makes slaves admire and revere their masters **52** *Fit I* I'd
better **54** *once* actually, after all

POET   Sir,
   Having often of your open bounty tasted,
   Hearing you were retired, your friends fall'n off,
   Whose thankless natures – O abhorrèd spirits! –
   Not all the whips of heaven are large enough –
   What, to you,   60
   Whose starlike nobleness gave life and influence
   To their whole being? – I am rapt, and cannot cover   62
   The monstrous bulk of this ingratitude
   With any size of words.   64

TIMON
   Let it go naked; men may see't the better.
   You that are honest, by being what you are
   Make them best seen and known.   67

PAINTER   He and myself
   Have traveled in the great show'r of your gifts,   68
   And sweetly felt it.

TIMON   Ay, you are honest men.

PAINTER
   We are hither come to offer you our service.   70

TIMON
   Most honest men! Why, how shall I requite you?
   Can you eat roots and drink cold water? No?

BOTH
   What we can do, we'll do, to do you service.

TIMON
   You're honest men. Ye've heard that I have gold?
   I am sure you have. Speak truth; you're honest men.

PAINTER
   So it is said, my noble lord; but therefore   76
   Came not my friend, nor I.

TIMON
   Good honest men! Thou draw'st a counterfeit   78

---

62 *rapt* bemused **64** *size of* number of – i.e., adequate **67** *them* i.e., the ingrates you speak of **68** *traveled in* experienced **76–77** *therefore / Came not* not for this reason came **78** *counterfeit* (1) portrait, (2) falsehood

Best in all Athens. Thou'rt indeed the best;
80 Thou counterfeit'st most lively.

PAINTER   So, so, my lord.

TIMON
E'en so, sir, as I say. *[To Poet]* And for thy fiction,
Why, thy verse swells with stuff so fine and smooth
83 That thou art even natural in thine art.
But for all this, my honest-natured friends,
I must needs say you have a little fault.
Marry, 'tis not monstrous in you; neither wish I
You take much pains to mend.

BOTH   Beseech your honor
To make it known to us.

TIMON   You'll take it ill.

BOTH
Most thankfully, my lord.

TIMON   Will you, indeed?

BOTH
90 Doubt it not, worthy lord.

TIMON
There's never a one of you but trusts a knave
That mightily deceives you.

BOTH   Do we, my lord?

TIMON
93 Ay, and you hear him cog, see him dissemble,
94 Know his gross patchery, love him, feed him,
95 Keep in your bosom; yet remain assured
96 That he's a made-up villain.

PAINTER
I know none such, my lord.

POET   Nor I.

---

80 *counterfeit'st* (1) paints, (2) fakes it; *lively* (1) in lifelike fashion, (2) actively 83 *thou . . . thine art* the products of your art are like nature itself (but *natural* also meant "like a born fool") 93 *cog* cheat 94 *patchery* roguery 95 *Keep . . . bosom* cherish him 96 *made-up* complete

TIMON

Look you, I love you well; I'll give you gold,
Rid me these villains from your companies.
Hang them or stab them, drown them in a draught,   100
Confound them by some course, and come to me,
I'll give you gold enough.

BOTH

Name them, my lord; let's know them.

TIMON

You that way, and you this, but two in company;   104
Each man apart, all single and alone,
Yet an arch-villain keeps him company.
    [To Painter]
If, where thou art, two villains shall not be,
Come not near him.
    [To Poet]   If thou wouldst not reside
But where one villain is, then him abandon. –
Hence, pack! There's gold; you came for gold, ye slaves. 110
    [To Painter]
You have work for me; there's payment.   111
Hence!
    [To Poet]
You are an alchemist; make gold of that. –   113
Out, rascal dogs!   *Exeunt [both, beaten out by Timon,*
                                who retires to his cave].
    Enter [Flavius the] Steward and two Senators.

STEWARD

It is vain that you would speak with Timon;
For he is set so only to himself   116
That nothing but himself which looks like man
Is friendly with him.

-----

100 *draught* privy   104–6 *You . . . company* i.e., wherever either of them
goes, a villain also goes   110 *pack* be off   111 *there's payment* (since Timon
now strikes him)   113 *alchemist* one who strives to transform base metals
into gold (i.e., one who strives by art to improve on nature); *that* (the blow
Timon now gives him as well)   116 *set . . . to* so completely wrapped up in

FIRST SENATOR   Bring us to his cave.
119   It is our part and promise to th' Athenians
120   To speak with Timon.
SECOND SENATOR   At all times alike
        Men are not still the same. 'Twas time and griefs
        That framed him thus. Time, with his fairer hand
        Offering the fortunes of his former days,
        The former man may make him. Bring us to him,
        And chance it as it may.
STEWARD   Here is his cave.
        Peace and content be here! Lord Timon! Timon!
        Look out, and speak to friends. Th' Athenians
        By two of their most reverend Senate greet thee.
        Speak to them, noble Timon.

        Enter Timon out of his cave.

TIMON
130   Thou sun that comforts, burn! Speak and be hanged!
        For each true word a blister, and each false
132   Be as a cauterizing to the root o' th' tongue,
        Consuming it with speaking!
FIRST SENATOR   Worthy Timon –
TIMON
        Of none but such as you, and you of Timon.
FIRST SENATOR
        The senators of Athens greet thee, Timon.
TIMON
        I thank them; and would send them back the plague,
        Could I but catch it for them.
FIRST SENATOR   O, forget
138   What we are sorry for ourselves in thee.
        The senators with one consent of love
140   Entreat thee back to Athens, who have thought
        On special dignities, which vacant lie
        For thy best use and wearing.

---

119 *part and promise* promised part   132 *cauterizing* searing with acid or a
hot iron   138 *What . . . thee* the wrongs we are sorry to have done you

SECOND SENATOR   They confess
  Toward thee forgetfulness too general-gross;
  Which now the public body, which doth seldom
  Play the recanter, feeling in itself
  A lack of Timon's aid, hath sense withal
  Of it own fall, restraining aid to Timon,   147
  And send forth us to make their sorrowed render,   148
  Together with a recompense more fruitful
  Than their offense can weigh down by the dram;   150
  Ay, even such heaps and sums of love and wealth
  As shall to thee blot out what wrongs were theirs   152
  And write in thee the figures of their love,   153
  Ever to read them thine.   154

TIMON   You witch me in it;
  Surprise me to the very brink of tears.
  Lend me a fool's heart and a woman's eyes,
  And I'll beweep these comforts, worthy senators.

FIRST SENATOR
  Therefore so please thee to return with us   158
  And of our Athens, thine and ours, to take
  The captainship, thou shalt be met with thanks,   160
  Allowed with absolute power, and thy good name   161
  Live with authority. So soon we shall drive back   162
  Of Alcibiades th' approaches wild,
  Who like a boar too savage doth root up
  His country's peace.

SECOND SENATOR   And shakes his threat'ning sword
  Against the walls of Athens.

FIRST SENATOR   Therefore, Timon –

TIMON
  Well, sir, I will; therefore I will, sir, thus:

---

147 *it own fall* its own decline   148 *sorrowed render* amends for regretted
wrongs   150 *can . . . dram* can, weighed scrupulously, outbalance   152
were theirs they did you   153 *write . . . figures* mark you with the signs,
proofs, or sum   154 *Ever . . . thine* thus providing a permanent record of
their esteem for you   158 *so* if it   161 *Allowed with* given   162 *Live with
authority* shall remain authoritative

If Alcibiades kill my countrymen,
Let Alcibiades know this of Timon,
170 That Timon cares not. But if he sack fair Athens
And take our goodly agèd men by th' beards,
Giving our holy virgins to the stain
173 Of contumelious, beastly, mad-brained war,
Then let him know (and tell him Timon speaks it
In pity of our agèd and our youth)
I cannot choose but tell him that I care not —
And let him take't at worst — for their knives care not,
178 While you have throats to answer. For myself,
179 There's not a whittle in th' unruly camp
180 But I do prize it at my love before
The reverend'st throat in Athens. So I leave you
182 To the protection of the prosperous gods,
183 As thieves to keepers.

STEWARD   Stay not; all's in vain.

TIMON
Why, I was writing of my epitaph.
It will be seen tomorrow. My long sickness
Of health and living now begins to mend,
187 And nothing brings me all things. Go, live still;
Be Alcibiades your plague, you his,
And last so long enough!

FIRST SENATOR   We speak in vain.

TIMON
190 But yet I love my country and am not
191 One that rejoices in the common wrack,
192 As common bruit doth put it.

FIRST SENATOR   That's well spoke.

TIMON
Commend me to my loving countrymen —

---

173 *contumelious* insolent   178 *answer* suffer the consequences   179 *whittle* knife   180 *at* in   182 *prosperous* propitious   183 *keepers* jailers   187 *nothing* oblivion, death   191 *wrack* ruin, waste   192 *bruit* rumor

FIRST SENATOR

These words become your lips as they pass through
them.

SECOND SENATOR

And enter in our ears like great triumphers
In their applauding gates.

TIMON   Commend me to them,
And tell them that, to ease them of their griefs,
Their fears of hostile strokes, their aches, losses,
Their pangs of love, with other incident throes   199
That nature's fragile vessel doth sustain   200
In life's uncertain voyage, I will some kindness do
them:
I'll teach them to prevent wild Alcibiades' wrath.   202

FIRST SENATOR

I like this well. He will return again.

TIMON

I have a tree which grows here in my close   204
That mine own use invites me to cut down,
And shortly must I fell it. Tell my friends,
Tell Athens, in the sequence of degree
From high to low throughout, that whoso please
To stop affliction, let him take his haste,
Come hither ere my tree hath felt the ax –   210
And hang himself! I pray you do my greeting.

STEWARD

Trouble him no further; thus you still shall find him.

TIMON

Come not to me again; but say to Athens,
Timon hath made his everlasting mansion
Upon the beachèd verge of the salt flood,   215
Who once a day with his embossèd froth   216
The turbulent surge shall cover. Thither come,

---

199 *incident* incidental   202 *prevent* anticipate   204 *in my close* i.e., along-
side my cave ("close" ordinarily meaning "enclosure," "yard")   215 *beachèd
verge of* beach that edges (is the limit of)   216 *embossèd* foaming

218   And let my gravestone be your oracle.
      Lips, let four words go by and language end.
220   What is amiss, plague and infection mend!
      Graves only be men's works, and death their gain.
      Sun, hide thy beams; Timon hath done his reign.

                        Exit Timon [into his cave].

FIRST SENATOR
      His discontents are unremovably
224   Coupled to nature.
SECOND SENATOR
      Our hope in him is dead. Let us return
      And strain what other means is left unto us
227   In our dear peril.
FIRST SENATOR   It requires swift foot.   *Exeunt.*

                       *

∽ **V.2** *Enter two other Senators with a Messenger.*

THIRD SENATOR
1   Thou hast painfully discovered; are his files
2   As full as thy report?
MESSENGER   I have spoke the least.
3   Besides, his expedition promises
4   Present approach.
FOURTH SENATOR
5   We stand much hazard if they bring not Timon.
MESSENGER
      I met a courier, one mine ancient friend;
7   Whom, though in general part we were opposed,
      Yet our old love made a particular force

---

218 *oracle* source of wisdom   224 *Coupled to nature* part and parcel of his being   227 *dear* grievous
    V.2 Before the walls of Athens   1 *painfully discovered* (1) learned with effort, (2) told us with distress; *files* ranks (of Alcibiades' army)   2 *spoke the least* given a conservative estimate   3 *expedition* speed   4 *Present* immediate   5 *they* (the senators, designated first and second, sent out for this purpose)   7 *general part* public affairs

And made us speak like friends. This man was riding
From Alcibiades to Timon's cave   10
With letters of entreaty, which imported
His fellowship i' th' cause against your city,
In part for his sake moved.   13
    Enter the other Senators [from Timon].

THIRD SENATOR   Here come our brothers.

FIRST SENATOR
No talk of Timon; nothing of him expect.
The enemy's drum is heard, and fearful scouring   15
Doth choke the air with dust. In, and prepare.
Ours is the fall, I fear; our foe's the snare.   *Exeunt.*   17

*

❧ **V.3** *Enter a Soldier in the woods, seeking Timon [for
    Alcibiades].*

SOLDIER
By all description this should be the place.
Who's here? Speak, ho! No answer? What is this?
    [Reads.]
"Timon is dead, who hath outstretched his span.
Some beast read this; there does not live a man."
Dead, sure, and this his grave. What's on this tomb
I cannot read; the character I'll take with wax.   6
Our captain hath in every figure skill,
An aged interpreter, though young in days.
Before proud Athens he's set down by this,
Whose fall the mark of his ambition is.   *Exit.*   10

*

---

13 *moved* undertaken   15 *scouring* scurrying about in preparation for battle
17 *Ours . . . snare* i.e., I fear we are about to fall into our enemy's trap
    V.3 Before Timon's cave   6 *cannot read* (apparently because in an unfa-
miliar language, as a Latin epitaph would be to an Elizabethan soldier); *character* lettering   10 *the mark . . . is* is his goal

✵ **V.4** *Trumpets sound. Enter Alcibiades with his Powers before Athens.*

ALCIBIADES
Sound to this coward and lascivious town
Our terrible approach.
    Sounds a parley. The Senators appear upon the walls.
Till now you have gone on and filled the time
4   With all licentious measure, making your wills
5   The scope of justice. Till now myself and such
As slept within the shadow of your power
7   Have wandered with our traversed arms and breathed
8   Our sufferance vainly. Now the time is flush,
9   When crouching marrow in the bearer strong
10   Cries, of itself, "No more!" Now breathless wrong
Shall sit and pant in your great chairs of ease,
12   And pursy insolence shall break his wind
With fear and horrid flight.

FIRST SENATOR   Noble and young,
14   When thy first griefs were but a mere conceit,
Ere thou hadst power or we had cause of fear,
We sent to thee, to give thy rages balm,
To wipe out our ingratitude with loves
Above their quantity.

SECOND SENATOR   So did we woo
Transformèd Timon to our city's love
20   By humble message and by promised means.
21   We were not all unkind, nor all deserve
The common stroke of war.

FIRST SENATOR   These walls of ours
Were not erected by their hands from whom

V.4 *Before the walls of Athens* **4** *all licentious measure* every form of licentiousness **5** *scope* determinants **7** *our traversed arms* our weapons crossed, as they would be during drills but not during battle **7–8** *breathed . . . vainly* spoken in vain of our sufferings **8** *flush* ripe **9** *crouching marrow* latent courage **12** *pursy* short-winded; *break . . . wind* fart **14** *conceit* fancy **21** *all* altogether

You have received your grief; nor are they such   24
That these great tow'rs, trophies, and schools should fall
For private faults in them.   26
SECOND SENATOR   Nor are they living
Who were the motives that you first went out.   27
Shame, that they wanted cunning, in excess   28
Hath broke their hearts. March, noble lord,
Into our city with thy banners spread.   30
By decimation and a tithèd death,   31
If thy revenges hunger for that food
Which nature loathes, take thou the destined tenth,
And by the hazard of the spotted die   34
Let die the spotted.   35
FIRST SENATOR   All have not offended.
For those that were, it is not square to take,   36
On those that are, revenge; crimes, like lands,
Are not inherited. Then, dear countryman,
Bring in thy ranks, but leave without thy rage;   39
Spare thy Athenian cradle, and those kin   40
Which in the bluster of thy wrath must fall
With those that have offended. Like a shepherd
Approach the fold and cull th' infected forth,
But kill not all together.
SECOND SENATOR   What thou wilt,
Thou rather shalt enforce it with thy smile
Than hew to't with thy sword.
FIRST SENATOR   Set but thy foot
Against our rampired gates and they shall ope,   47
So thou wilt send thy gentle heart before   48
To say thou'lt enter friendly.

---

24 *they* (those who caused your grief)   **26** *them* those who wronged you   **27** *the motives . . . out* responsible for your original banishment   **28** *Shame . . . excess* excessive shame over their folly   **31** *tithèd death* death to every tenth person (an explanation of *decimation*)   **34** *die* (singular of dice)   **35** *die the spotted* perish the guilty   **36** *square* just   **39** *without* outside   **47** *rampired* barricaded   **48** *So* if only

SECOND SENATOR   Throw thy glove,
50   Or any token of thine honor else,
      That thou wilt use the wars as thy redress
52   And not as our confusion, all thy powers
      Shall make their harbor in our town till we
54   Have sealed thy full desire.
ALCIBIADES   Then there's my glove;
55   Descend, and open your uncharg̀ed ports.
      Those enemies of Timon's and mine own
      Whom you yourselves shall set out for reproof
58   Fall, and no more; and, to atone your fears
59   With my more noble meaning, not a man
60   Shall pass his quarter or offend the stream
      Of regular justice in your city's bounds
62   But shall be remedied to your public laws
63   At heaviest answer.
BOTH   'Tis most nobly spoken.
ALCIBIADES
      Descend, and keep your words.
        *[The Senators descend and open the gates.] Enter
        [Soldier as] a Messenger.*
MESSENGER
      My noble general, Timon is dead,
      Entombed upon the very hem o' th' sea,
67   And on his gravestone this insculpture, which
      With wax I brought away, whose soft impression
69   Interprets for my poor ignorance.
ALCIBIADES   *Reads the epitaph.*
70   "Here lies a wretched corpse, of wretched soul bereft;

---

52 *confusion* ruin   54 *sealed* completely satisfied   55 *uncharg̀ed* unattacked;
ports gates   58 *atone* appease   59 *meaning* intentions   59–60 *not . . . quarter* not one of my soldiers shall leave his prescribed duty area   62 *remedied*
handed over for redress or punishment   63 *At heaviest answer* for severest
punishment   67 *insculpture* inscription   69 *Interprets . . . ignorance* will
yield you the meaning which I am too ignorant to get from it (cf. V.3.5–8
and V.3.6n.)   70–73 *Here . . . gait* (one of these two contradictory couplets
was possibly meant for cancellation)

Seek not my name. A plague consume you wicked
    caitiffs left!
Here lie I, Timon, who alive all living men did hate.
Pass by and curse thy fill; but pass, and stay not here   73
    thy gait."

These well express in thee thy latter spirits.
Though thou abhorr'dst in us our human griefs,
Scorn'dst our brains' flow and those our droplets which   76
From niggard nature fall, yet rich conceit   77
Taught thee to make vast Neptune weep for aye
On thy low grave, on faults forgiven. Dead
Is noble Timon, of whose memory   80
Hereafter more. Bring me into your city,
And I will use the olive with my sword,   82
Make war breed peace, make peace stint war, make each   83
Prescribe to other, as each other's leech.   84
Let our drums strike.   *Exeunt.*

---

73 *gait* steps 76 *brains' flow* tears 77 *niggard* (since our tears are *droplets*
indeed when compared with the seas that now wash Timon's grave); *conceit*
imagination 82 *use . . . sword* combine peace with war 83 *stint* stop 84
leech physician

AVAILABLE FROM PENGUIN CLASSICS

THE PELICAN SHAKESPEARE

Hamlet • King Lear • Macbeth

A Midsummer Night's Dream • Romeo and Juliet • Twelfth Night

General Editors: Stephen Orgel and A. R. Braunmuller

New Illustrated Covers designed by Manuja Waldia